Buddha

Sri Nisargadatta Maharaj

Avadhut Nityananda

The Nirvana Sutras
and
Adavaita-Vedanta

The Nirvana Sutras and Adavaita-Vedanta

Beneath the Illusion of Being

*The Essence of Buddhism
and the essence of Advaita-Vedanta
are so identical that they can no longer
be kept separate from one another.*

*The illusion of consciousness
is the illusion that you are.
It is the illusion of being.*

Dedication

Avadhut Nityananda

Nisargadatta Maharaj

Sakyamuni Buddha arguably
the world's greatest teacher

Nagarunja the father of Madhyamika
(middle way) Buddhism

To the memory of my former editor, Greg Sawin,
whose work on *You Are Not* and *Walden III*
was exceptional

Acknowledgements

Jacques Derrida: the father of Postmodernism

Alfred Korzybski: Father of General Semantics

Andrea Isaacs for her persistant, detailed
and quality editing

Matthew Greenblatt for his direct feedback

My Divine Leani

Dingeman Boot, Meinhard Van de Reep
and Alexander Smit for providing me
with photos of Nisargadatta Maharaj.

*How can "I"
speak of something
which does not
exist*

Getting Warmed Up

*There is no self, "I," inner self, soul,
present time or presence.*

> **When there is no-I there is Nirvana.**
> **— Buddha**

When my teacher Nisargadatta Maharaj was confronted by a student who said, "I just want to be happy," Maharaj said, *"That's nonsense, happiness is where the "I" isn't."*

The personal "I" is a *mirage* which does not know it is a *mirage.* To try to reform, or transform this non-existent entity some call *sadhana* (spiritual

practice) but it is like trying to make a better, more compassionate, clearer, more aware, healthier or more mindful *mirage*. Some call this *mirage, maya,* others the illusion. By whatever name, the illusion includes all perceivables, experiencables, and conceivables. To understand this is to go
BENEATH THE ILLUSION OF BEING.

There is no inner self just a universal SELF which is consciousness it*self*. Once the illusion of the personal self and inner self disappears, all problems and manifestations are seen as universal consciousness that is SELF realization. Nirvana means extinction, whereby there is no longer a self or even a universal consciousness.

Prior to the Nirvana Sutras

*R*eturning to *Walden III* is quite ludicrous since there is no *Walden III*, no Utopia, nor is there a Nirvana. Continuing this process means looking at the glue that holds together "spirituality" as well as "psychology" which is hinged on the belief or illusion of a being that exists and the reality of the *subject-I.*

The quotation marks around "I" and other words are used to emphasize the non-existence of the quoted word. The quoted word is an abstraction made of "nothing" produced by the nervous system and hence suggests its non-existence. Without the abstraction process and the vehicle of language, neither the *subject-I,* nor the philosophy that it expounds would be possible.

This text as a follow-up to *Walden III* focuses on the *crème de la crème* of the last 2500 years of science and spirituality, deconstructs and demonstrates to the reader that there is no "I" upon which "spirituality," or "psychology" is based.

The **Nirvana sutras and Advaita-Vedanta** are aimed to strike at the heart of the central delusion which holds together all "spiritual" and "psychological" paths; it is the belief in the existence of a *subject "I," a being, or a self.* To **realize** that there is no separate independent individual subject-"I" or self with choice, volition and an independent self-nature liberates the number one confusion from the psycho-spiritual industry that has plagued us from the beginning of time through this postmodern era. Addressing the misconception that there is an independent, separate, individual, "subject-I", self or being, presence, or soul can bring us beyond the postmodern era to the age of **post-deconstruction,** which is beyond the need to heal, repair, reform, transform or liberate this nonexistent entity called "I."

My teacher Nisargadatta Maharaj said, "You will not get any benefit from theses teachings; these teachings are beyond benefits."

The Nirvana Sutras and Advaita-Vedanta grafts together 2500 years of science, spirituality, philosophy and research to produce an understanding that the basic initial **illusion** is that there actually exists a *subject I,* a being "inside." The problem is the illusion that there is a self which is choosing and running the show. This problem escalates once the reality of the "I" is taken to be real and tries to heal or transform the *subject-I* into something better or more "spiritual." The non-existent *subject-I* must be "seen" for what it is—an abstracted representation of **nothing.**

It is truly unfortunate, but once the belief in the abstraction of existence, in a being or self is imagined to be true, it becomes the foundation for the further production of even more inaccurate abstractions, representations, and pain.

Please note this is not a text for the weak of heart. Rather, it demonstrates that not only is there no *Walden III* or Nirvana, but, there is no **subject-I**, *self or soul* upon which to base "spirituality" or "psychology."

Unfasten your seatbelts

With Love
Your brother
Stephen

The Nirvana Sutras and Advaita-Vedanta Made Simple
A Summary

1. The *subject -I* is formed by the psychological abstraction process which creates language and which carries with it the illusion of separation (Territories) and the illusion of "individuality."

2. Language and speech are the vehicles which form the understanding of what we call Eastern and Western spirituality and psychology. It can be said that all language, by its sound, produces the illusion of a separate object with a territory or boundaries which did not exist prior to the abstraction process.

3. What the nervous system allows us to perceive is an abstracted sensory map of an object, not the object itself, i.e., we see a map of the object. The nervous system produces an abstract map which is a representation of something that is not there. Hence, arbitrary sounds which form **words produce representations of things — not actual things but abstracted representations of things which are not there.** Nisargadatta Maharaj called these abstracted representations, concepts. For example, when I say the word **"book,"** the word and sound image **"book"**

produce the illusion of a separate object within its own territory creating the illusion of boundaries and a separate individual existence.

4. As a more "personal" example, the words "I," me, mine, called the ego, and the great problems of "spirituality" and "psychology" are sounds and word images that carry with them the illusion of territorialized separate subjects (separate from other territorialized subjects) with an origin, location or place of departure, and **the illusion of being** the source of their existence and what they perceive or imagine they perceive. This contributes to the illusion of both an existence and an identity separate from other subjects.

5. These illusions are deconstructed by Buddha's *Diamond Sutra* some 2500 years ago: *"There is no world," "There is no separate individual self nature"*, therefore *"Forsake all Dharmas"*, and later by Madhyamika Buddhism's founder Nagarjuna, with two simple words, *__dependent arising__*, meaning nothing originates by its own separate individual will or existence.

6. This illusion of separate territorialized or boundaried existence is further deconstructed in the Quantum physics of the middle 1960s by John Stuart Bell with his theorem (Bell's Theorem) which states, **"There is no location"**, and hence **there are no local causes**.

7. Even more recently, the noted philosopher and architect of postmodernism, Jacques Derrida's use of Ferdanand de Saussure and Ludwig Wittgenstein's understandings which demonstrate that there is no original source or existence prior to words. Spiritual paths which describe a world and a subject-"I" naturally use words. This places boundaries or territories which create **the illusion of a separate individual** *subject-I* **that has a path,** a *subject-I* with a separate location, along with the ultimate misunderstandings, the imagined existence of a place, space, permanent state or goal called nirvana.

Why then, with so much proof of the nonexistence of an independent, separate, individual *subject-I*, does the nonexistent *subject-I* remain the focal point and origin of all psycho-spirituality?

This question "I" cannot answer; however, "I" can say that language is the great territorializor producing the illusion of a *subject-I* which, if it realizes its own nonexistence, disappears.

Religions are based on the resistance to the disappearance of the *subject-I* which is viewed as death by producing other worlds, or other incarnations. To realize that there is no *subject-I*, "self" or "being" is to kill the linguistic (philosophical) map of the *subject-I* and therefore (the illusion of) one's self.

To dismantle the illusion of a *subject I*, we begin with "understanding" and end with nothing. "Form is emptiness, emptiness is form" (the Buddhist Heart Sutra), or as in the eastern traditions of Buddhism and Advaita-Vedanta, I AM THAT– YOU ARE NOT

Definitions

1. *Nirvana* means extinction or annihilation The Buddha simply denies there is a subject.

2. *Advaita* means one substance, not two.

3. *Vedanta,* for practicable purposes, means *neti-neti,* Sanskrit for "not this, not that.

4. **Self**: a separate, individual, independent entity with free will, and volition.

5. **Presence**: the existence and or experience, often times referring to a God that is prior to the existence of a self or experiencer.

6. **Soul:** an invisible immortal part of a man or woman distinguished from the body, which lives on after death.

7. **Illusion**: something that appears to exist but does not.

8. **Chaos**: complete confusion, formless void before the creation of the universe (Webster Dictionary); the infinity of space or formless matter

supposed to have preceded the existence of the ordered universe (American College Dictionary).

9. **Faith**: The belief in something without proof of its existence.

10. *Sutra*: literally means a thread. A sutra is a short pithy statement that can generally not be understood without a commentary. For our purposes, a Sutra is a sentence that can encapsulate volumes of material. It can take years of meditation to penetrate its meaning.

In the context of this text, several different approaches will be utilized so that the clarity that there is **no *subject-I*, being, soul or self** will become inescapable. Each **sutra** is followed by a short commentary. Its purpose is to lead the reader step by step through the understanding that there is no separate, individual, independent being, subject-I or self so "one" can go *BENEATH THE ILLUSION OF BEING* into the substratum or underlying substance that everything is made of, which we will call undifferentiated, consciousness, or the substance.

The reader is advised to focus on each sutra until its meaning is revealed.

When "there is no "I" is realized," that is nirvana

Nirvana is an arbitrary sound signifying a word which represents or points to what is left after the realization that there is no subject-I, self or being, and the subsequent death of our postmodern era, and the birth of the era of post-deconstruction.

*W*e will use the term ***post-deconstruction*** to describe the process of using several different approaches to demonstrate the *illusion of being*. The Nirvana sutras combine many different texts from many different traditions called in some high brow circles "inter(*text*)ualization" of spirituality which catapults us beyond spirituality and into *the substance which ultimately is NOT*. The aim of the Nirvana Sutras is to demonstrate that the origin, root, jumping off point, of all psychology and spirituality is based on a non-existent fictional entity called the *subject-I*. Once this is **realized,** pain collapses as do the spiritual and psychological systems that are organized around something called an **ego** or "I" which does not exist.

Sutra 1: Spirituality and psychology are based on the subject-I, and therefore all psychology and "spirituality" are "I" dependent.

Commentary

*I*t should come as no surprise that the illusion that the *"subject-I"* actually exists is the basic premise, the starting off point, the root of both spirituality and psychology, because if there was no *subject-I,* no separate being or self, there would be nothing to heal and no ego to be gotten rid of.

If there is no *subject-I*, then there is no spirituality and there is no personal psychology.

In order to appreciate this, the **Nirvana Sutras** will demonstrate that the subject, the "I", the "I AM", the self, the *jiva*, the *purusha*, and even the witness are illusions to be discarded.

Some might be lead to believe the subject-"I" is responsible for its actions and has free will. This is like saying that a water droplet which appears in the ocean is responsible for its appearance, its actions and has volition and choices as to where and in what direction it goes. The water droplet, like the "I", appeared and it will disappear, and that is the long and short of it.

Sutra ii: The organizing illusion is the belief in the existence of a separate individual independent subject-I, a being, an ego or self.

Commentary

*T*he greatest problem in discovering "who you are" is the belief that there is a self, a being a subject-I. This misunderstanding that there is a separate, individual, independent subject-I which exists at all is the **organizing misunderstanding.** Once the existence in a subject-I, self, being, etc. is presumed to be true, all other misconceptions and pain follow. Therefore, to attack this central **organizing illusion** through "understanding" that the true obstacle is the assumed, unquestioned place of departure on any psychological or spiritual path is to attack the belief *that you* are.

Sutra iii: *Psychology and spirituality are based on the illusion of a separate independent self, and in its more advanced delusional stages it becomes the belief in a non-existent "higher self", transpersonal self, or a universal self to overcome the "lower self."*

Commentary

ew could argue that the history of psycho-spirituality is hinged on the *subject-I's* existence; without a *subject-I*, there would be no psychology or spirituality. Psychology and spirituality are dependent on the existence of an independent, individual, separate self or *subject-I*. The proof of this lies in on-going attempts to improve, transform, heal, make healthy, a more loving, compassionate, forgiving, tolerant, pure, aware or even mindful *subject-I*.

This becomes more subtle as a separate "higher subject-I" called the "higher self," the soul, the observer, and even the witness, awarer, knower, "higher self," "transpersonal self," or even a universal self is formed. These notions presuppose a separate witness who witnesses and a separate self who is witnessed.

This attempt at self-improvement or even integration to overcome or transform some "lower self" into some "higher self" with holy ideas and idealized behaviors that the self should become in order to become an enlightened *subject-I*, self witness or observer goes on through every type of process from meditation, fasting, yoga, therapy, and body-work, and demonstrates the depth of this delusion. For now, we not only have a non-existent self, but once society steps in the **"I" splits itself in two**. Society's standards from religion and parents become the idealized "higher self" and the biological animal self becomes the lower self. Thus, the *illusioned* self now develops two parts, always in conflict in an eternal battle. Some schools even create and validate this battle with archetypical realms and stories which serve to only mystify and further *illusion* us.

Some religions even create a society of monks in India called swamis which take a vow of poverty (owning only two clothes), begging for food, called *biksha*, and renouncing all worldly possessions thus claiming their status as closer to God, when actually it is only the aggrandizing of the lot of the very poor, making poverty a virtue and begging a sacrament, (see *Walden III*, **slave virtue**).

This process is so large that in the 21st century, both psychology and spirituality have become not only a lifestyle but an industry with licenses, codes of behavior, certificates, lineages and successors to validate and justify their existence.

All psychology and spirituality are based on the belief that both the **_subject I_ exists,** and also a "higher" **_subject I_**. In addition, there has been a belief in the existence of a **_subject I_** as separate, with an independent individual existence with choices, volition, a will, a history, with sins and virtues and with a past, a present and a future that creates this reality

Sutra iv: Sadhana (spiritual practice) is an attempt to reform or transform a non-existent self or subject-I.

Commentary

Most spiritual practice is about trying to reform or transform a nonexistent entity; this attempt some call *Sadhana (spiritual practice).*

Each psycho-spiritual system or meta-physical system (meta meaning beyond, hence metaphysical meaning beyond the physical) is devised to help comfort, heal, transform and improve the *subject-I,* self or soul in its imagined journey to become "higher", "better", or more "spiritual in the spiritual game and more healthy, wealthy and wise in the psychological game.

But what if there was no separate ego, *subject-I,* self or soul. What if the jumping off point, the *subject I,* self or soul was not, and a "higher" self was not. What if the *subject-I* were a construction of the nervous system, an illusion produced through the nervous system's abstracting process, a by-product produced by the coming together of fluids called neurotransmitters and nothing more.

Sutra v: No "I" means the death of the psycho-spiritual business.

Commentary

When the belief in the existence of the *Subject-I* disappears, it leads to the collapse of spiritual and psychological systems, businesses, and an industry. "We" would then be forced to re-evaluate, where "we" were, where "we" are, who "we" are and where "we" are going. More importantly, it might help us to *understand* why after generations of psycho-spiritual self-improvement programs and paths, for the most part, we were given a new philosophy built on the illusion of a nonexistent subject or ego called "I." This could be likened to building a spiritual or psychological world based on nothing, and once this is **realized**, like a house of cards it all collapses.

Nobel Prize winning author Albert Camus said, "*A leap of faith is a leap of fear.*" If all the psycho-spiritual assumptions which depend upon a nonexistent *subject I*, self, or soul were not valid, then we would be in a *leap of fear* and hence trapped in *the illusion of a non-existent entity, an illusion of being.* *The illusion of being* is founded upon information that has been passed down for generations, later becoming learned thoughts fused with perception, and finally yielding what is commonly called individual experiences. It is the illusion of a perceiver "seeing" what is not there through this learning-perception-experience mechanism that in India they call *maya*.

Sutra vi: Nirvana means extinction.

Commentary

Nirvana is an arbitrary sound signifying a word which
represents or points to what is left after the realization
that there is no subject-I.

Nirvana can be defined as both extinction
and/or annihilation. At first blush, it
seems outrageous that the history of spirituality
would end with extinction. However, what better
way to describe the death of ego or **the death of
the illusion of a separate ego** then with annihilation. It sounds funny at first that for thousands of
years people were unknowingly seeking annihilation. But what else could **the death of the illusion
of "I"** point to?

There has been an illusion for thousands of
years that an ego or "I" enters nirvana. Rather,
there is actually no "I", being or self, to be annihi-
lated or to enter Nirvana. In other words, there was
never an "I" to begin with.

"No being has ever entered Nirvana"
(Buddha)

Sutra vii: The "I" gives the illusion of being; go beneath the illusion of being.

Commentary

In order to approach this, we will use the neti-neti (not this, not that) of Vedanta, which is called dismantling in Quantum Psychology, the deconstructive understandings of Buddhism, tantric yoga, quantum physics, neuro-biology, Western philosophy, linguistics, postmodernism, Hindu Yoga and Jnana Yoga, and Advaita-Vedanta. These approaches have one thing in common at their core: they deconstruct the belief that there is an "I" and by doing so, they lead us *beneath the illusion that there is a being* which is nirvana, and into *you are not*. In this way, *as* the one substance, these vehicles reach the same climax.

Sutra viii: Nothing is.

Commentary

This understanding is subsumed under the great work of the Greek Sophist, Gorgias, about 2500 years ago. Gorgias had three major statements.

1) Nothing exists.
2) If it does exist, it cannot be known.
3) If it's known, it cannot be communicated.

Through these three sutra-like statements, Gorgias (500 B.C.) melds the East and the West with the purest form of Buddhism (500 B.C.), tantric yoga, Advaita-Vedanta and 21ˢᵗ century science.

It is Gorgias who breaks through the illusion of meaning in order to begin to peal the layers of the onion back and go **beneath the illusion** to find that there is nothing there.

Fortunately, or unfortunately for the reader, as we utilize all of these approaches to demonstrate that there is no-I upon which to base psychology or spirituality, we must include two approaches which are the most difficult to grasp: 1) **there is no** *subject-I on a biological level,* and 2) *the "I" exists in language only.* But first a very brief overview of all of the eight approaches.

Sutra ix: Everything is consciousness; nothing exists outside of consciousness.

Commentary

antric yoga says that everything in the universe is made of undifferentiated consciousness. Although not purely tantric, this has been stated in the ancient text *The Yoga Vashishta,* when Vashishta (the Guru) says to Ram (the student) that "everything is consciousness, nothing exists outside of consciousness." However, even in *The Yoga Vashishta,* often times we are left with a dualistic understanding rather than an understanding that there is only *that one substance.*

In the **tantric** texts of Kashmir, however, *everything is consciousness* and consciousness is depicted as Shiva. Unfortunately more common than not, people misinterpret this to mean that they or a *subject-I* or some self or being is Shiva or will *become* universal consciousness, a universal "I", witness or subject, and upon doing so will *become* something. Rather then confronting the self or "I" with the understanding that *everything is consciousness* means even the subject-I, or witness is consciousness.

This means five very powerful and yet distinct things:

- First, what you see, for example this book, is not a book made of consciousness, rather it is consciousness as, or in the form of a book.

- Second, since everything is made of consciousness, there is no subject-I, there is only consciousness; hence, the knower, reader, or witness of the book is made of the same consciousness or substance as the book.

- Third, since the knower (of the book) and the known (the book) are made of the same consciousness, there is no knower or known since both are the same substance.

- Fourth, since everything is consciousness, nothing exists outside of consciousness. Not only is there no individual self, there is not separate individual mind.

- Fifth, there is no consciousness, because in order to recognize everything as consciousness, there must be something to say this is so. Since even the witness of consciousness is consciousness, then there is no witness. With no witness there is nobody to say everything is consciousness; hence, *there is no consciousness.*

In practice, Tantric approaches (to be discussed later) vary from most other approaches in one key way—**UTILIZATION**. Except for Quantum Psychology which both deconstructs and utilizes, most other approaches only deconstruct, discard or dismantle (not this—not that); only tantric approaches **utilize** all experiences including them as *and this and this.*

Sutra x: There is only one substance, not two—discard all as Not This, Not That.

Commentary

The second approach is called *Advaita-Vedanta*. *Advaita-Vedanta* has two basic principles. First, there is only one substance, not two, and second, *neti neti,* translated from the Sanskrit as "not this, not that." It is the negation and dismantling of everything that leads ultimately to the realization of *the one substance. In this deconstructive or dismantling process,* there is no "I", and everything is one substance. But again, as in Tantric Yoga, ultimately there can not be a one substance unless there is an "I"/self/witness/awarer to say it is so. Hence, the ultimate neti-neti is discarding the **subject-I** in all its different forms including its perception of the one substance.

Sutra xi: The Buddhist Heart Sutra: "Form is none other than emptiness, emptiness is none other than form."

Commentary

The third approach is Buddhism. Buddhism has such an extraordinary history of deconstruction with the emphasis on *no "I"*, that to do it justice, I will further subdivide it into several sub-sutras. When I say Buddhism, "I" do not mean what is being taught in 99% of current Buddhist teaching. "I" am talking about what distinguishes Buddhism from Hinduism.

Sutra xi-a: there is no separate individual soul or self that incarnates again and again and again.

Commentary

Buddha was a Hindu and Hinduism believes in an individual soul or self, which incarnates from lifetime to lifetime to lifetime. Buddhism is Hinduism reformed. Buddha's realization under the Bodhi Tree about 2500 years ago states, *there is no separate individual soul or self that incarnates again and again and again.* This realization that there is only *one substance*, which he calls *emptiness, describes what is not.* Buddha states it clearly in the **Heart Sutra**: **"Form is none other than emptiness, emptiness is none other than form. "** We could say then that everything is emptiness (everything

IS NOT); we could say that what *is not* is form. But ultimately what the Buddha would say is that everything is *sunyata*. *Sunyata* does not mean void (which is also an experience requiring a *subject I*), rather it means *not even form or emptiness*.

"Emptiness is the relinquishing of all views. For whomever emptiness is a view, that one will accomplish nothing."

This is reminiscent of the man who goes to the Zen Master and says, "My friend is always experiencing emptiness; what advice can you give him?" The master replies, "Tell him to give up the emptiness."

Sutra xi-b: "there is no world," therefore "forsake all Dharmas" (The Diamond Sutra).

Commentary

"There is no world," therefore "forsake all Dharmas." "There is no independent origination" (all is an interconnected whole), also called by Nagarjuna *"dependent arising"* (all is dependent on all that occurs). Since "there is no separate individual independent self nature," then a separate individual independent self does not exist, or is empty (*is not*). In other words, there is no self which has an individual, independent, separate existence.

Nagarjuna, the Father of middle way Buddhism (2nd century), goes even further in saying since everything is empty of independent self-existence, therefore a self IS NOT, *and a separate individual mind is not.* He said, *"There never was a Buddha who ever taught anything."* This explains why Buddha never really spoke of Nirvana; because if the void voids itself, there is no void and there is no *Nirvana.* This is *Nirvana as extinction.*

Sutra xi-c: We cannot describe what is the real nature of everything because this nature is beyond all description, beyond all conceptualization, beyond all dualities.

Commentary

*D*ovetailing with the neti-neti of Advaita-Vedanta, Buddhism suggests that a separate independent nature called a self or a thing is not. We can say that as everything is connected to everything else which as said in Nagarjunas' dependent origination is the key to the Buddha's teaching. Once we see the dependent origination that there is no independent individual separate self nature, we will no longer believe in separate existence. And since there is no existence, the self whose definition must include a separate independent individual existence *is not*, hence the self is empty of self existence. That is Nirvana.

In a nutshell, everything that is dependently originated is necessarily empty of inherent separate individual independent self existence.

Ultimately, dependent origination, like emptiness, is also empty of inherent existence. Dependent origination, like emptiness, should be seen as part of the temporary raft, a mere tool, not as an absolute.

Nothing at all exists separate
of anything else, because everything
is dependently originated, then
everything is empty of
inherent separate, individual,
independent existence.

Sutra xi-d: All dharmas or elements of existence are Sunyata, or void.

Commentary

*T*he Prajnaparamita (or perfection of wisdom) which contains *The Heart Sutra* and the short Vajrachchedika (literally, "Diamond Cutter," commonly called Diamond Sutra), share the same themes. According to these sutras, all dharmas or elements of existence are Sunyata, or void. If one understands Sunyata, the Voidness of the Void, one recognizes that it is not a "nothing" one knows or can imagine or perceive.

Clarifying Some Definitions

Emptiness is an abstract idea representing impermanence, unreality, instability, transience, and relativity in the nature of all existence. All phenomena and the ego have no reality, but are composed of a certain number of elements, called *skandas* which disintegrate. In Buddhism like in Quantum physics, everything is unstable, e.g. electrons jumping from one orbit to another and forming new atoms and molecules, possess no self-essence, volition, will or self-nature, i.e., everything's existence is dependent on the conditions of everything's existence. Therefore there is no separate, independent, individual self, or we could say the self is empty; it is not.

Even in the subatomic world there are no specific atoms—each atom is connected to all other atoms and they have no separate independent individual self-nature other than through the eyes of a perceiver.

Sutra xi-e: The "I" and the universe are composed of an interaction of the elements or skandas.

Commentary

"Skanda" is a Buddhist word that literally means a group, in this case the group of component parts which as a whole comprise personality.

Buddhism states quite clearly that the personality is a play of the skandas:

Form/matter: firm, fluid, hot, cold and having movement

Sensation: unpleasant, pleasant, neutral

Perceptions: form, sound, smell, taste, bodily impressions and mental objects

Mental formations: volition, attention, discrimination, attention, joy, happiness, equanimity, resolve, exertion, concentration, compulsion

Consciousness: seeing, hearing, smelling, tasting, bodily sensation and mental consciousness

In this way there is no "I" or ultimate entity that exists outside of the skandas, but rather the concept of a self with or as an independent, separate, individual entity is an illusion.

NOTE: The skandas are a _perception_ which requires an "I" to perceive it.

Considering all of the above, there is no Buddhism, but rather there is what the Buddha said before Buddhism became an institution and Buddhism became a lifestyle. Therefore, throughout this text, the focus will be on what the Buddha said, not how to live a Buddhist life style. Distinguishing what Buddha said from what is being taught is reminiscent of the famous words of Carl Jung: "Thank God I'm Carl Jung and not a Jungian," or as the Buddha might say if he were alive today, "Thank God I am the Buddha and not a Buddhist."

Sutra xii: Everything including the perceiver of the world is an abstracted representation of nothing. *THIS IS NOT A BOOK.*

Commentary

*T*he fourth approach is **neurobiology**: *the world and "I" as an abstraction of nothing.* Let us first begin with nothingness, which is not even nothingness. To illustrate, let us imagine that we could expand the size of the nucleus of an atom to the size of the sun and an electron to the size of the earth. In this scenario, there would be more empty space between the nucleus and the electron then there actually is between the earth and the sun.

The nervous system abstracts (omits and selects out) leaving an estimated .000054% omitting all of the emptiness and selecting out only a small fraction thus producing the illusion of solidness, for example, **A book**.

These abstracted remaining fragments of information are discontinuous but the nervous system produces a continuous *illusion* of an *"I"* and later a projected self, world, book, or being as solid, stable and constant, with story-like explanations, in a meta (big) narrative or "spiritual" story.

The nervous system thus creates the illusion of a continuous, unfragmented *"I"*, which appears through the abstraction process as a whole.

On a practical level, this fragmentation explains why one minute you are thinking about three years ago, the next dinner tonight, and the next minute where I will go on holiday. Each fragment is *grafted* together along with the idea of an "I" with a unified existence. History, as Michel Foucault and biology as Gilles Deleuze would say, produces this misunderstanding of a solid, stable self rather than a fragmented discontinuous self. This is why in India one of the most famous meditations is to find the space between two thoughts, or what Jacques Derrida calls the dissemination point where two texts are grafted together.

From a Kashmir Shavite (tantric) point of view, this discontinuous self appears and disappears and appears and disappears in what in Sanskrit is called **spanda, translated as "the divine throb," or "the divine pulsation."**

This tendency to form *the illusion of a whole* unfragmented continuous world, self, or "I" creates *the illusion of continuity,* wholeness, an actual "perception" of a separate mind and a universe which has a source point or logos called self or God. We then see that what Advaita-Vedanta would call concepts, neurobiology calls abstracted representations and sound calls words and language are all representations of things and are discontinuous.

The illusion of the perception that the mind is a container for perceptions, such as a solid stable world, a book or an "I", appears to us through the vehicle of the nervous system. *The "I", the perceiver of the "world," arises after an action or event has already occurred.* The perceiver-"I" *illusions doership* for an action or event which has already occurred before the perceiver-"I" was even produced, or the perceiver was present to even perceive the event.

The *subject-I*, as an abstracted representation of nothing, appears by the neurological movement of fluids called neurotransmitters which carry abstracted information by omitting billions of stimuli and selecting out only a small fraction estimated at .000054% of what is perceived. The "*subject-perceiver-I* is literally *thrown into the world* claiming doership, choosership, authorship and volition for actions and events that occurred before it was even produced by the fluids of the brain and nervous system. More fascinating is that the nervous system keeps reconstituting the "I" so as to maintain a homeostatic self-contained unit. This homeostatic automatic reproduction of the "I" by the nervous system gives the "I" the **illusion of being and the illusion of a perceptual apparatus called a mind** existing in time as if it actually existed prior to the movement of fluids which yield the abstracted experience of a subject-I, self or world.

Sutra xiii: The nervous system and the mind operate on binaries.

Commentary

Whether we are discussing yoga, duality, the perception of a dualistic mind or

Postmodern binary relationships, few could dispute that the nervous system imagines a vehicle called a "mind" which views the world and itself in terms of binaries. For example, you (your nervous system) sees *this, not that,* i.e., this is good, that is bad, this is closer to God, that is further away.

Moreover, when any term or experience is focused on, the nervous system forces the opposite to appear as if it's not there. For example, when an "I" perceives a feeling of love, the feeling of hate moves outside of awareness to the *margins,* or when an "I" perceives a book, the perception of the chair you are sitting on moves to the perimeter of the perceiver's perception.

Sutra xiv: *The* great way is easy except for those who have preferences (*Zen Patrich*).

Commentary

*A*s mentioned in Sutra xiii, it is the habit of the nervous system to experience and perceive one thing, and omit its opposite. This results in three tendencies: 1) the nervous system *marginalizes* one of the words or experiences, i.e., perceives love, and omits hate; 2) the nervous system gives preference to one experience over another, i.e., love is good, hate is bad; and 3) the nervous system assumes one of the experiences is closer or further away from God, i.e., love is a quality of god, and hate takes us further away.

We can begin to appreciate that the nervous system is binary which means it perceives or produces a perception of **this, not that.** It perceives love and moves hate outside of its awareness and into the *margins* as if it is non-existent, and it <u>learns</u> to **prefer** one experience, in this case love, over another experience called hate, judging it to be closer or further away from the source, God, also called the logos. Advaita Vedanta, on the other hand, discards both as **neti-neti,** meaning *not this, not that.* Tantric yoga sees both love and hate as being made of the same consciousness, thereby including all (in this case love and hate) with **and this, and that.**

Meditate on everything, including the witness, or "I" as made of the same energy or consciousness.

In Wittgenstein's rabbit picture we see either a rabbit or a duck. We cannot see both of them at the same time. In the same way the nervous system "sees" this not that.

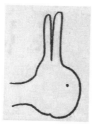 

Wittgenstein's rabbit pictorial

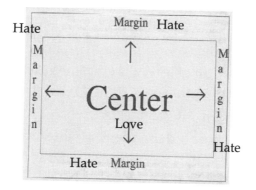

Declaring a localized center pushes its opposite to the margins.
De-construction is smashing a center and its margins.

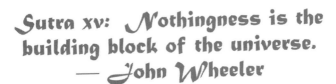

Sutra xv: Nothingness is the building block of the universe.
— John Wheeler

Commentary

The fifth approach is quantum physics. We can begin by noticing how Einstein's historic statement, "Everything is made of emptiness and form is condensed emptiness", echoes The Buddhist Heart Sutra, "Form is emptiness, emptiness is form. "We can also notice how David Bohm's "Everything is an interconnected whole," echoes not only Nagarjuna's **dependent arising** but also Advaita's **One substance.** When all of this is explored in the light of **Bell's theorem, "There are no local causes, and there is no location (non-locality),"** it is no wonder how "*the cause of all things is the cause of all things,*" along with John Wheeler's statement, "*Nothingness is the building block of the universe.*" These bring into a quantum focus what Nisargadatta Maharaj said to me, "Now you know the nothing, and so now you can leave."

Sutra xvi: There is no I, just an interaction of sub-atomic particles in a constant play or dance.

Commentary

A physicist might say that all that we see as solid is actually at another level the interaction of subatomic particles where no separate "I" with a will, a volition or choice even exists.

Sutra xvii: "I" am not the doer."

Commentary

*Y*oga, Sanskrit for union or "to yoke," is the sixth approach, and generally implies the duality of two or more substances. However, even though yoga text implies there are two substances, it implicitly suggests one substance which it refers to as "Brahman," the *word principle* of which and from which all arises and is made of. Moreover, as mentioned in *Sutra ix*, The Yoga Vasishta says, *"Everything is consciousness, nothing exists outside of consciousness."* Certainly this is where at its core and essence, traditional eight limbed yoga meets the rather controversial tantic yoga. What remains unfortunate is that all too often this common underlying principle goes unseen as traditional yoga is referred to as the **right**-handed path and tantric the **left**-handed path. This rather curious way of calling traditional yoga the **right** and tantric the **left** refers also to the fact that in India, there is no toilet paper, so the left hand is used.

More unfortunate is that the two parts of Yoga pertaining to the underlying substance and no-"I" remain neglected as the "spiritual practice with its rules and judgments about high and low and pure and impure are emphasized rather then the underlying unity.

That there is no "I" with volition or choices, can easily be understood as portrayed in the *Bhagavad Gita* in two ways. First, everything occurs and is a play (interaction) of the elements, air, earth, water, fire, and ether where even the "I" is an illusion whose appearance comes as an interaction or play of the elements. In this way, the "I" is made of the five elements and hence has no doership. Second, all is a play (interaction) of the gunas or forces — Sattva (purity), Rajas (action) and tamas (inertia). Here also there is no "I" with volition, rather the "I" is made of and is subject to these forces.

Somehow this understanding of no "I" and the underlying one substance is neglected when it should be emphasized. To illustrate this *no-I* and no volition or doership point, Nisargadatta Maharaj said to me, "even the physical form of the Guru (a liberated being) is subject to the play of the gunas."

Sutra xviii: The universe and the "I" are brought about by an interaction of the physics dimensions and forces.

Commentary

Quantum Psychology, in *The Way of the Human, Vol. III* states that the physics dimensions and forces, i.e., energy, space, mass, time, electro-magnetics, gravity, light, sound, dark matter, the strong force and the weak force, all interact to form what are commonly called archetypes. Spiritual paths, along with the "I," are ultimately formed through an interaction of the forces and dimensions. For Quantum Psychology and post-deconstruction, there is no "I" or spirituality prior to this condensed play of the forces and dimensions.

Sutra xix: The "I" is a representation of nothing.

Commentary

The "I" is an abstracted representation, a reproduction, a *map*, produced by the nervous system through an abstracting process whereby approximately .000054% remains after this abstraction process.

In other words, when we see a *book*, the nervous system is making a map in the brain of a *book* by omitting more than 99.99% of the empty space to form this solid *book* map or illusion. Actually, *there is no book there*, just a map made of nothing projected "outward" which produces the *book* illusion that is perceived. Hence the sub-title, *This is Not a Book*.

$\mathcal{S}$utra xx: $\mathcal{T}$he "I" exists in language only.

Commentary

The seventh approach is postmodernism which contains the linguistics of Ferderand de Saussaure and the philosophy of Ludwig Wittgenstein. Postmodernism or post-structuralism arrived around 1967 and was presented initially by **Jacques Derrida**, the notorious French philosopher who began to deconstruct all of the language in Western philosophy. Derrida took the understandings of Ferderand de Saussaure (the father of linguistics and semiology), and the anthropologist Claude Levi-Strauss (who understood that language functions via binaries whereby the first term is aggrandized over the second term), and Ludwig Wittgenstein who understood that all exists in language as a *language game.* Derrida deconstructs both language and binaries through his important insight into the force of *Differ̲ance* (difference with an "a" to be discussed next).

Sutra xxi: Words have meaning only in relation to other words, but not outside of the abstsracted context of language-map-metaphor in which they are being used.

Commentary

Derrida uses the word differance (differ-ence with an "a") to demonstrate that what words mean <u>refers</u> to other words, which refers to other words, but in the end, meaning always depends on other words, and hence you can never get to "the meaning", and there is no meaning outside of linguistic symbols and signs outside of language.

In any language system, every word which is called a signifier functions by referring to other words (signifiers) without ever arriving at what the word represents which is called a signified). This is true because not only is language an abstracted representation; what language represents is also an abstracted representation. *This language game cre-*

ates the illusion of actual things which have an independent existence prior to the abstraction or representation-language process.

Words and sounds are arbitrary (Saussure), their meaning determined by their use (Wittgenstein). The meaning of language is determined by differences in sound signifiers. For example, the differences between <u>c</u>at and <u>b</u>at and <u>s</u>at are determined by the first consonant.

What seems obvious, but it was only stated by Saussaure, is that the words we use are arbitrary and are determined by the culture. For example, "water" in English, "agua" in Spanish. More importantly however, these words have no meaning outside of their usage (Wittgenstein). In other words, all words are arbitrary (have no **universal** meaning outside of their usage), cultural (different language, English, Spanish etc., for the same word), and meaning is dependent upon how it is used in relation to other words, but **there is no actual separate thing which exists outside or prior to how it is used in language. Language is an abstraction which represents itself, not an actual independent thing which exists outside of words.**

To directly relate this to our understanding, all experiences and what they mean are determined by culture, language and use. For example, I had a friend of mine 30+ years ago who was dating a neurologist in the early 1970s. One day she had an experience of having no boundaries; she felt One with everything. When she told me, I thought, "Far-out, obviously a 'spiritual experience'." Her boyfriend had her examined by a psychiatrist who diagnosed her as having a dissociative disorder. Again, the meaning of experiences is determined by the context, culture and language.

Sutra xxii: *Words are names for things which have no separate independent or even actual existence outside of the perceiver's perceptual experience.*

Commentary

Saussare overturns Plato when he says, **there are no ready-made ideas which exist outside of language. This means there are no ideal forms or perfect ideas like Justice (with a capital J) which exist prior to language in some "other" world.** Thoughts are words or signs which name or represent things that have no existence outside of language and whose meaning is deferred (can only be determined through the use of other words).

Moreover, the *subject-I* is produced as a representation of the nervous system abstracted out of nothing after the action or perception has already occurred.

What are signs? Signs are symbols that represent things. A sign, however, is a representation, a sound that can only represent itself; it is a verbal abstracted map, not a pre-absracted thing which actually exists. A sign can only represent itself as a word within a language system or culture; outside of the system of signs or words of the culture, the sign becomes meaningless (outside of a culture that does not possess those same signs).

Sutra xxiii: The sign as a representation, represents a thing which has no existence prior to its representation.

Commentary

*A*rbitrary sounds which become signs give the *illusion of having a pre-existence prior to words.* The signified, that which the sign represents, is also an *abstraction perceived by a perceiver.* The existence of the thing perceived is **perceiver dependent.** In this way, the sign is arbitrary (cultural) with no existence prior to words.

More importantly, that which the word signifies is an abstracted representation which has no existence outside of a perceiver, and hence no independent original self nature or presence (presence meaning an existence prior to words).

Nothing exists as a separate individual entity but rather as an entity or map based on the nervous system of the *perceiver-I*, or the abstracted system of language. For this reason Wittgenstein called this a *language game.*

This is one meaning of the Buddha's, *"There is no separate individual self nature."* There is no presence or pre-existing separate thing which exists prior to words. To state again, **a word does not represent a thing; a word represents a concept or map of a thing.** *Remember the nervous system abstracts leaving only an estimated .000054%. From nothing, the nervous system makes a map or concept of a **book**, but this is not a book. Actually there is no **book** outside of the nervous system's abstracted map or concept.*

Sutra xxiv: You do not see an object, you see a map or concept of an object. This leaves us with the notion that what we see actually exists.

Commentary

What we see are abstracted representations of nothing. We live in the illusion that what we see is a representation of something out there. This could imply that there is something out there and that you see a representation of it. This is

Thu Aug 2-12 4:42pm
Acct: 1103 Inv: 104696 D 00
Don Fallu

Qty	Price Disc		Total Tax

9780974995403 The Nirvana Surtas & Advai
| 1 | 18.95 | | 18.95 a |

| | Subtotal | | 18.95 |
| | a HST | 5% | 0.95 |

Items	1 Total		19.90
	Cash		20.00
	Change Due		0.10

======== Frequent Buyer Status =========
Credit earned with this purchase $ 0.95
Total credit on your account.... $ 10.68
Credit is available for future purchases

Returns require this receipt

incorrect. *There is nothing out there.* What is seen out there is an abstraction of NOTHING, and I don't mean nothingness as a thing.

Moreover, the "You" who sees an object is not something that is "in here." Both the perceiver (seer) and the perceived (seen) are abstractions of NOTHINGNESS. What you call "You" is actually made of nothingness condensed. *There is nothing "in here."*

Sutra xxv: *"There is nothing external to the text;" we are the text we are deconstructing.*

Commentary

This sutra is the famous statement by Derrida and represents *The Heart Sutra of Postmodernism.* **We are the text we are deconstructing.**

In neurology, the "I" is produced after the event and action have taken place, and is an abstraction of the nervous system.

Since all language is sound, and language is

text, the "I" which exists in language only is text. The *Neti-Neti* of Advaita-Vedanta would discard the text, in this case the "I," as language itself, as the text.

The understanding that there is no "I" in Advaita-Vedanta can be considered the same as:

- in Buddhism, there is no separate independent individual self (since all separation is linguistic, and in language);

- in Madhyamika Buddhism, there is no independent origination, source or self nature outside of language which of course overlaps with

- David Bohm's interconnected wholeness in Quantum Physics, and

- neurophysiology's "all perceivables exist only as an abstraction of nothing."

Hence text (language), which includes the "I", is an abstraction of nothing.

In this way, when Postmodernism is expanded greatly, we can utilize it in all eight approaches to illustrate the true meaning of "*the death of the illusion of the subject-I*" as it pertains to **nirvana as extinction.**

Sutra xxvi: There is only the text. No readymade ideas exist before words.

Commentary

There is an illusion that somewhere in another world there is **Real Virtue or Real Justice** with a capital **V** or **J**. However, there is no justice or virtue that exists outside of language or outside of how the culture determines its meaning.

Moreover, the text also includes the "I", the awarer, observer, witness, perceiver, recorder of the text, which is an experience and so requires an experiencer; as such, it is an abstraction in language and in text. The experience of being, as subject, is a perceivable, experiential abstraction. The *subject-I* is part of language or the text. Each element of language is part of or a supplement of another word or element of language. It is the difference in sound that produces language, and the"I". *It is only in sound or language that the subject-I exists.* **The "I" is a supplement of the text.**

Sutra xxvii: "The cause of bondage is sound."
—Siva Sutras

Commentary

The "I" is a by-product of sound which forms language. The *subject-I* is a supplement that is dependent on the relationship and function of other sounds and words. The "I" is a map or concept that is always *under erasure* (to be discussed later). Therefore the perception and experience of "I" is sound and word dependent, and as such it is the "cause" of *the illusion of bondage.*

Moreover, since sound forms letters and letters form words and words form text or concepts or the "I", "the "cause" of bondage is sound."

Sutra xxviii: There is no presence, present, or pre-existence prior to memory or words.

Commentary

> "There is no presence or present" is the backbone of both Buddhism as well as Postmodernism.

*T*he belief in a separate individual thing with a presence or an existence outside of language and the abstraction process colors and adds to *the illusion of an "I" or being which exists prior to abstraction, perception and language. The illusion that there is an existence of an actual independent thing in present-time outside of or prior to abstraction or perception is at the root of our confusion/illusion.*

If we are *illusioned* into believing that each word actually represents an independent thing which has an independent separate existence outside of perception and language, then we are asleep to the fact that the "I" is a word, which is an abstracted representation of nothing. Moreover, when we accept that the "I" has no existence outside of language, on a perceptual/thinking language level, we then realize that **absence** (as part of the presence/absence binary) becomes marginalized and in spiritual circles made more valuable. Both emptiness and form are perceptual experiences and as such the aggrandizing of one (emptiness) over the other (form), keeps the spiritual illusions of language and perception alive. In this way we must include both equally (form and emptiness) in order to deconstruct both as NOT. Therefore, any process of deconstruction must include:

"What is being left out?"

"What is being resisted?"

"What is being suppressed?"

"What is being denied?"

Each of these questions brings forth its marginalized opposite and aids in dissolving the binary process of the nervous system that aggrandizes one term, experience or perception over another. Since the experience being aggrandized (in this case absence or emptiness) is at the center to deconstruct, the process of including both sides of any polarity in postmodernism is called de-centering. This aggrandizes one term, such as love, or a value like compassion, or an experience like seeing blue light, over another term, such as hate or passion.

In order to de-center (include both sides of a polarity), and deconstruct the illusion of an independent existence, we must "get" absence as the pre-cursor to presence and hence shift the binary from presence/absence to absence/presence and then deconstruct both. As the next step "we" can deconstruct both the illusion of presence and the illusion of absence, because both are "I"/perceiver dependent, and as such are non-existent abstractions *dependently arising* ("arising together," Nagarunja), producing the illusion of a present or absent self.

Sutra xxix: **There is no present-time that can be experienced. All perceptions and experiences are in the past as memory.**

Commentary

Everything we see is an abstraction. The perceiver arises after the event has occurred. What the perceiver perceives has already occurred, and the perception of experiences and what they mean arise after the experience has already occurred. If we define memory as seeing and/or experiencing something which is from the past, then anything which is perceived, has already occurred, is in the past and is a memory.

Sutra xxx: The force of differance (difference with an "a") holds the illusion of the existence prior to words of the "I."

Commentary

*D*ifference (difference with an "a") is a force structured by the "tracks" of language. Differance deconstructs not only the illusion of an "I" which exists somehow outside of or prior to language but also validates the most basic tenet of Buddhism, *no thing exists as a separate independent permanent entity which is separate from other things.* As the "I" exists in language in relationship to other words, realizing its **dependent abstracted existence** is an aid in deconstruction, or in Vedanta terms, *Neti-Neti.*

"We ourselves are the text we are deconstructing."

Sutra xxxi: Sound which becomes signifiers represents nothing.

Commentary

// ... *T*here is no thing in itself outside of the network of referral in which signs function (Of Grammatology, pages 48-50)."

Differance is a description of a linguistic tendency, and hence a tendency which creates differences and defers meaning. It is intrinsic to the world and a glue which holds together the "I" along with the mirage of thought fused with perception.

All theoretical models fall apart with differance as they are seen as a *language game, a theory that exists in words but has no existence outside of words.* In this way we are always returning to a network of words where meaning is "always already" postponed, deferred and canceled. This is the *Neti-Neti* of Advaita-Vedanta.

"There is nothing outside the text" tells us that "realization" takes place via *not this–not that*, as language is discarded.

Sutra xxxii: All words should be put Under Erasure (neti–neti).

Commentary

The term and process called "<u>under erasure</u>" was coined by Martin Heideggar, the noted philosopher and author of *Being in Time* (1927). Heideggar would write a word, like BEING, as such ~~BEING~~, thus freeing it from a fixed origin. In actuality, this entire book could be placed under erasure.

One sign leads to another and so on indefinitely. Psychology, or having a personal psychology or mind is a metaphor, as is the story of spirituality, having an "I" or ego or mind to overcome. This is simply a *language game*. Saying "It's my mind," is a metaphor, a figure of speech that people have taken to be true. Once this is understood, psychology and spirituality become a *theory of abstracted words or signs rather than a theory of things which actually exist.* For example, the theory of religion or psychology or the idea of manifestation is a *language game of words* with no actual existence outside of words and no actual self (self being defined as a separate, independent, individual entity) with a separate independent individual self-existence. Every word has to be put under erasure: words have escaped the main inquiry. In other words, words or signs are *illusioned* to represent real things. All experiences are based on a perceiver and language and an "I" which are all abstractions. **Therefore, all theories, be they psychological or spiritual, are a theory of signs not things.**

"At each step I was obliged to proceed...letting go of each concept" (XVIII preface of Grammatogy).

Derrida via Heideggar, like Buddha in the *Diamond Sutra* (forsake all dharmas), places all absolute theories under erasure. The **Nirvana sutras** understand that the void is also an experience and as such the void voids itself, it erases itself, and is NOT, along with erasing differance.

> The Buddha taught that there is no substantial essence underlying and supporting the manifest world.

The problem lies within each word, for it is each word that gives **the illusion of a pre-existing thing that exists outside of perception and language.** This is the illusion of presence and a logos (a pre-existing source or cause) creating the illusion of a separate independent thing which exists prior to abstractions and later, words. Moreover, it is the suppression of the awareness of differance, that produces **the illusion of a self that is independent, with a presence (existence prior to the abstraction process) and a logos (a source or cause generally considered to even have a location) which exist outside of abstraction/perception and language.**

The discourse of the text or the *Langue* (Saussaure) is the structure of language prior to the "I" or thought which produces ideas; this too is text. Thoughts and the "I" word or signs occur through the suppression of the awareness of differance.

In Madhyamika Buddhism and Advaita-Vedanta, all of this is to be discarded as **Not This–Not That** (Neti-Neti). However, even the discard<u>er</u> is part of **the discourse or text of enlightenment,** which is a spiritual discourse and metaphor which is to be discarded (Nisargadatta Maharaj).

Erasing points of view, frames of reference and points to locate from...leaves us with the no-state state of the non-being-being of Quantum Psychology, and later post-deconstruction, stated in words as: *no frames of reference, no references to frame.*

Sutra xxxiii: *The search for a logos, a source, a center, a beginning, a cause, a path is hardwired into the nervous system and contained within language. This process is based upon the abstraction process and the illusions of language.*

Commentary

The history of philosophy is the history of a search for a logos, an originary source or presence which is pure and beyond the physical world, says **Jacques Derrida**. Moreover, psychology's history is a history of the search for a **cause** which acts as a logos to explain an illusionary presence and heal an illusionary self (Wolinsky).

History and psychology seek a logos (cause) to explain a continuity of change when in fact both history and psychology are laden with breaks, ruptures and leaps and are discontinuous, attempting to organize the chaos, and support and promote meaning where none exists (Wolinsky/Fouccault).

It cannot be overstated that *impermanence,* a basic tenet of Buddhism, fits as the cornerstone of the abstracting process because it is the abstracting process which creates **the *illusion of permanence.*** Moreover, at a subatomic quantum level, prior to the formation of the "I," a witness, or a self, there is constant subatomic change which goes unnoticed to the abstracted perceiver's perception.

It is the nervous system's abstracting process which creates through omission the illusion of a whole (gestalt) where none exist which leads to the production of a big metaphysical story and explanation.

This means that anything, including experiences, belongs to thoughts and a perceiver and are hence part of the **perceiver/experiencer discourse.** This illusion imagines an abstracted map to have an independent separate individual self-nature and a world with a **logocentric origin.**

One of the purposes of the nervous system is to organize chaos, and it does this through abstraction (suppression) and repression.

The search for a logos, a cause, a location is produced by the nervous system and is perceived as necessary. The abstracted "I" is produced by the nervous system after the event and action has occurred along with the "I's" illusion that it (the "I") decided to perceive a cause and a logos when actually it happened to the "I." This aids in the I's illusion of continued survival through the illusion of control.

Logocentric behavior and logocentric drive is a drive to find the center, source, the origin or cause of everything and is hardwired into the nervous system as a way (path) to organize chaos, and hence survive. It should be noted that not only does the nervous system seek to organize chaos, but in its attempt to do so, produces an "I" as an abstracted representation of **nothing** which imagines not only cause and effect but also that it (the *subject-I*) has an origin or is an originator or creator with a location in space-time that originates, creates or actually is the source of its thoughts, memories, emotions, associations, perceptions, and intensions. This is an *illusion of the nervous system.*

What is important to realize is that although the **logo-centric drive** initially was to find the source point for **survival** reasons only, i.e., God, that source point has always changed location. Initially the source was "up there" (in heaven or some other world), outside of us and created everything. Today, most new age philosophies have an "in here" or "down here" attitude, in what psychology calls the subject, the "I" or the ego, as if a self, being or higher self as somehow responsible for creating its own "external" universe.

Through the vehicle of language, and the illusion of pre-existence prior to abstraction and perception, people now imagine and have an anthropromorphic logos, a **logos** which gives a **"gift,"** or teaches lessons. Today, even companies who in the past had a desire to grow, expand and make money have reframed (now called "spin") this desire using the word **mission**, or **mission** statement, or a **calling**, all of which imply a separate logos, with a plan, a design, or a mission here on a separate earth.

East and West have both suffered from this **logo centric drive** because the drive to organize chaos and **survive** seems to be hard wired into the nervous system. In the west via Socrates-Plato-Descartes and later modern psychology, in the East *not* by Advaita-Vedanta, Tantric yoga or what Buddha said, but by what they have been _de_formed, not transformed into.

It is the operating of this biological logo-centric drive which leads us to believe that if we somehow find the **permanent** origin, the **permanent** source, the **cause or** point, call it God, then everything will be answered, and we will **survive** (*be saved* from death), not condemned (damned) to die.

This resistance to death with all of its stories of souls and heaven and hell and life everlasting is an outgrowth of this **survival** mechanism.

Sutra xxxiv: The logos has no location, it is non-local.

Commentary

Through the vehicle of Quantum Physics and Bell's Theorem (there is no location or local causes), *the logos has no location, i.e., it is non-local*. Although this non-local one substance (call it consciousness) is found in many approaches, it is generally not seriously understood in spirituality. Why? Because if the purpose of the nervous system is to organize chaos, then the drive to find a logos (a local source or course) is hard-wired into the nervous system which habitually searches for causes (sources) of pain (existence) so as to imagine itself or a logos which exists in a point somewhere to be the source or originator of the universe, with a reason, plan and lessons. This **survival** drive to find a logos coupled with the *anthropomorphic* tendency to project qualities of a nervous system onto things which have no nervous system has formed what is commonly called spirituality and psychology and which misleads with promises of permanent pleasure and freedom from pain.

Sutra xxxv: *"Do not think you will necessarily be aware of your own enlightenment."* — Zen Master Dogen-zenji

Commentary

The abstracted "I" which seeks a localized God (the logos) and an enlightenment as a state (referent) exist as a perception, a representation of **nothing, a sensation or** as words in language only. Therefore, since realization is that there is no-I, *"Do not think you will necessarily be aware of your own enlightenment"* (*Zen Master Dogen-zenji*).

Why? Because the "I" is produced from fluids (biological level), is an abstraction of the nervous system and as such the *subject-I* arises after the action event or perception has already taken place and exists in language only. The "I" is a by-product of the nervous system, an abstracted representation of *nothing* which arises after the action has already occurred, which is a learned thought or description.

The illusion is that there will be an "I" which gets enlightened or an "I" which becomes en-

lightened. With no-I there can be no-I that it even knows it is enlightened.

"Nobeing has ever entered Nirvana." — Buddha

Sutra xxxvi: There is no origin source or originary presence.

Commentary

All of the approaches in the Nirvana Sutras have several primary features in common.

First, there is no origin, source or originary presence, meaning there is no pre-existing thing prior to the abstraction process and sound being produced (trance-duced) by the brain into words.

Second, the total annihilation of the subject or what we call the "I. "

Third, as Advaita-Vedanta sees time and space as a concept, so postmodernism sees time and space as being a construction of language, Quantum Psychology sees time and space via linguistics, and biology as being an abstracted representation of nothing.

Fourth, As the Buddha said, "The question of a beginning is unanswerable; as Nagarjuna said, "There is no beginning there is no end." Throughout all of the spiritual traditions, we begin to notice that there is always a deconstruction, a dismantling, a discarding of everything *neti-neti* or "being seen" as empty (as not) including the concept of Truth with a capital "T." In post-deconstruction, Truth with a capital "T" is a big abstracted story used to explain everything. This process gives the illusion of a philosophy of a truth beyond the physical (metaphysical) which in the Nirvana Sutras is seen as Wittgenstein's *language games.*

Sutra xxxvii: Spirituality and psychology are abstracted representations of nothing and exist in language only, as a language game.

Commentary

All theories exist in language only and have no reality outside of words and language. To add a neurological twist, language is a descriptive representation, an abstraction of nothing. Theories of philosophy, spirituality, psychology and even science are abstracted representations of nothing representing nothing, and as such exist in language only.

Even experiences are perceptions and as such are abstractions of nothing.

Sutra xxxviii: The Nirvana sutras mix contexts to demonstrate that the root of spirituality and psychology is based on the belief in a non-existent subject-l.

Commentary

*T*he Nirvana sutras link "past" with "present" and "present" with "future," mixing con(*texts*) to hopefully enhance the understanding that all spirituality is based on a non-existent self which needs to be saved or transformed in some way.

This can be done because time, as an abstracted by-product of language, is a word which represents a thing that only exists as long as there is a perceiver there to perceive it.

With no time outside of a perceiver's perception, texts which are in language, as is "I," mix spiritual texts of past with the spiritual texts of present. This (inter)**text**(uality) can be seen in every form of psycho-spiritual development, all of which have no origin but rather intermingle (inter(**text**)ualize) everything that is said and done.

The *nirvana sutras* intermingle (inter(**text**) ualize) the ancient Advaita-Vedanta (text), with Buddhism's *Heart and Diamond Sutra* (text), Nagarjuna's Madhyamika Buddhism (**text**), Neurophysiology (**text**), Quantum Physics (**text**), Tantric Yoga (**text**) and the linguistic text of structuralism and post-structuralism termed postmodernism (**text**), with the deconstructive process to show us how the *grafting* of **texts,** i.e., inter(**text**)ualization, provides a "**new text**" by including spirituality and psychology and yet it takes us beyond that *one substance* of which the **text** is made and yet paradoxically is NOT.

For the sake of linguistic and textual ease, we will term this *Post deconstruction,* the inter(**text**)ualization of spirituality which catapults us beyond Postmodernism itself to *the substance which is NOT.* The aim of the Nirvana sutras is to demonstrate that the origin, root, jumping off point, of all psychology and spirituality is based on a non-existent entity. Once this is **realized** all pain collapses as does the spiritual and psychological systems or games called paths that are organized around something called an "I" which does not exist. It should be noted that all spiritual and psychological systems, called paths, are hardwired into the nervous system as a way to organize chaos and aid in survival. This drive for a logos actually has neurological pathways, within the brain.

Sutra xxxix: The self is made of abstracted words which are sewn together.

Commentary

What we call a self or a point of reference is an abstracted representation of nothing. It is a combination of different abstracted texts (words) or identities sewn together. These texts are discursive structures which combine to form the illusion of an "I" (subject).

There is no "I" outside of *learned* thought/word abstractions combined with perception, and there is no "I" outside these texts. In Quantum Psychology, there was no "I" outside of the false core-false self I-dentities. Unfortunately, people imagine an "I" which exists separate to and prior to these "I"-dentities or texts. **Prior to these "I"-dentities or texts there is no "I."** The "I" is constructed by the nervous system through the movement of fluids as an abstraction of sensation. Prior to the "I" there are sensations. To illustrate, let's imagine that the "I" appears and becomes aware that it is hungry and the "I" sees an image of a sandwich. The illusion is that the "I" **had** the image of the sandwich, when actually the "I" and the sandwich image arose together to aid in the nervous system survival.

In this way, the self which is imagined to exist separate, beyond, and prior to a text (in this case sandwich) is an imaginary self or "I" which was produced through fluids. Even the *I AM* is an abstracted thought which is part of the text. Even though non-verbal, the *I AM* exists as a part of information that we have received and hence remains a discourse and part of a subtle *language game.* If we exchange the word "information" for "knowledge" it becomes easy to appreciate the *Siva Sutras* *"Knowledge is bondage,"* as all knowledge comes from outside, or as Nisargadatta said, "All knowledge comes from outside, therefore discard it."

The self or "I" is (inter)text(ual) or a mixture of texts (discourses or discursive structures) which are sewn together like patchwork and which exists in language only. Hence the subject-I is nonexistent prior to words.

To deconstruct is to dismantle the I-dentities or texts means the disappearance of the "I" along with the text.

Sutra xl: The concept of "other" exists in language only.

Commentary

One of the great illusions of this abstracted representation we call language is that all language presupposes "other." Once the silence deepens and language falls to the background, there is no other.

All language has contained within it an illusory "I" and "other" that the "I" is refering to. Once those (the "I" and the "other") are seen as just a sentence, and then as made of the same substance along with the witness of the sentence, then everything disappears.

Sutra xli: What is, does not exist.

Commentary

In linguistics, the sound which *stands in* for a word is called a signifier and the thing it represents is called the signified. The illusion is that there is an object, for example, **a book,** that is actually in your hands. Actually, **the book** is not an object, but an abstracted map of a book, an abstraction of nothing, which only represents a thing, a book that is not there prior to the perceiver; this book is called the signified.

Two understandings need to be remembered. First, the sound or signifier is arbitrary, it has no inherent significance. For example, a sound like "virtue" or a **book** is called virtue or **book** respectively for no special reason. Second, The signif<u>ied</u>, the **book** itself, does not exist. Why? Because the signif<u>ied</u> **book** is an abstracted-representation of nothing.

Therefore, the sound (**book**) is an abstraction of nothing and the sound represents nothing, but an illusion of a something, **book** or virtue which has no existence, or independent separate self-nature outside of the nervous system's abstracting process.

Sutra xlii: The "I" is a linquistic effect of differance, (difference with an a).

Commentary

*F*or post-deconstruction, there no self or unconscious mind, only sound patterned by language and speech as abstracted by the brain and nervous system. Moreover, since the "I" is made of sound patterns without an origin, the "I" sound patterned by language and abstracted by the nervous system is formed by differance (words which refer to other words) and the suppression of *sound*s *in order to form language and speech.* Therefore the "I" is an experience produced by a suppression of the realization of differences in sound which produces language. **The "I" is a linguistic effect of the process called differance:** *This means that for an "I" to believe in its existence outside of language there must be a suppression of the realization of the force of differance The "I" must imagine it is not part of a linguistic pattern formed by words with its meaning derived by differance, but rather must imagine itself with an actual separate independent individual existence prior to and separate from language.*

Sutra xliii: Sound has no origin.

Commentary

Sound is only there as long as a nervous system hears it — otherwise there is no<u>thing</u>.

This leads to the death of the *illusion of presence,* presence being defined as the existence of a thing prior to the abstraction process. Since all perceivables and later words which describe perceivables are abstractions of nothing, words do not stand for objects but rather stand-in for abstracted representations of nothing which appear as objects and ideas. *The cause of bondage is sound (Siva Sutras).*

Sutra xliv: There are no pre-existing or ready-made ideas prior to words (Saussaure).

Commentary

*A*ll words and spiritual ideas represent things and principles which do not exist prior to the abstracting process and language. *The illusion is that somehow there are spiritual ideals and principles that exist prior to words; spirituality is an abstracted spiritual language game.*

As all words are an abstraction of nothing, and as all words or ideas can only represent abstractions of nothing, this leaves us with *Buddha's basic premise that there is no separate individual self nature. Why? Because the self is linguistic, an abstraction and a perception which means it can not*

be by itself, or without everything else. This deconstructs Plato's belief in a presence, essence, perfect
ideas, pre-abstracted universal forms, holy ideas
or even archetypes as described by Jung, as actual
"things" *in another world or collective* that exist outside of words.

Sutra xlv: The "I" has no existence outside of the abstraction process which produces words and language.

Commentary

*L*et us begin here with Wittgenstein and his
use of **language games**. If the "I" exists in
language only (which means it does not exist without an abstraction process which yields language)
and there is no "I," presence or transcendental existence separate from the word "I," then in any
language game and production of language, the
"I", observ<u>er</u>, perceiver, witness or awar<u>er</u> is part
of the language game itself. There is no preexis-
tent "I" that exists prior to the word "I. " *The "I"*

is part of a language game and becomes a discourse for which and from which the "I" is a by-product, with its meaning being determined solely upon how the word "I" is used. The "I" contains no self nature (separate, independent, individual pre-existence); *the "I" does not have an existence outside of the word "I. "* The "I" is a verbal abstraction produced by fluids, (neurotransmitters in the brain). There is no "I" outside of **learned** thought or language which gives "I" *the illusion of a presence and a learned location*. The "I" exists as a **learned response,** arises after the event or action has occurred and is made of condensed nothingness (Physics-Buddhism-linguistics). It is made of the same substance as everything else (Tantra-Advaita), and is not (Advaita-Vedanta-Madhyamika Buddhism)

Sutra xlvi: The experience of being, and being the subject is a learned response reinforced by thought which gets fused with perception.

Commentary

*B*eing the subject in a perceptual location is a learned experience/response, and since the perceiver is made of and produced by fluids and is an abstraction of nothing, so too all experiences and what they are and mean are learned thoughts coupled with perceptions. They reflect how the nervous system is organized and are based on its abstracting process. *The illusion is that this learned process of an "I" reinforced by thought exists in a specific location.*

Sutra xlvii: All experiences are abstracted representations of nothing.

Commentary

All experiences, even spiritual experiences and psychological insights, are nervous system dependent; as such they are perceptions and abstracted representations whose meaning is learned. The unfortunate part is that more often then not spiritual experiences and psychological insights are seen as important and given significance in some way rather then as a perception of an abstraction. This is naturally followed by the desire for the experience of enlightenment as a permanent state of never-ending pleasure.

Sutra xlviii: There is no doer, there is no author.

Commentary

Roland Barthes, in his article "The Death of the Author," demonstrates two drastic understandings: first, that the *subject-I*, author, authority or even the word of God in the case of the Bible, cannot be the source or origin of what it writes or speaks. Because the "I", as well as the author as subject exists as an abstraction, in language, with no existence outside of language. *The illusion of doership or authorship is an abstraction, a by-product of language, and as such doership or authorship is part of the language system.* There is no doer or author separate from language, and there is no doer or author separate from its discourse. The author is a by-product of the nervous system's abstraction process which is a by-product of language, like the "I," and as such is part of language, not separate from it.

Sutra xlix: There is no "I" or "other" separate from the discourse, language game, or language itself.

Commentary

From another vantage point, the "I," "writer," "author," appears after the writing has already occurred. Since the author appears after the writing has occurred (biological), the author then takes credit, doership, or authorship (Advaita Vedanta). For this reason, noted author Mallarne says, "It is language which speaks, not the author...[language] acts, not me" (*Death of the Author*, Roland Barthes, page 143).

Sutra l: The subject-l is a simulation of nothing.

Commentary

*I*n order to traverse postmodernism, we must begin with the word **simulation** as made famous by Jean Baudrillard, the high priest of Postmodernism.

Simulation is a copy of a copy of a copy which has no origin or original existence. According to Baudrillard, this forms a **hyper-reality** or a model that is no longer based on a simulation but which has nothing to do with the simulation itself.

At first this might seem complicated but is actually quite simple. To illustrate, let's imagine a town in your city. This town is a similar copy of another earlier town, which carries characteristics of other earlier more primitive towns going back to the caves.

Each progressive copy is a copy of a copy. Easy, so what? However, there is no original town of towns or "Archecopy" because prior to caves maybe we were apes who lived in trees, birds, or one-celled animals who were once carbon, oxygen, hydrogen, nitrogen, phosphorus, etc. Again, so what? So there's no original.

If we start from this implied beginning, we can see **everything is a copy of everything else with no original**. This means that there is an *illusion which exists in language that leaves the impression of a beginning in time. But if it goes back to nothing prior to the perceiver, then there is no being or original anything which exists outside of the implications and illusions which are contained within language itself.* There are no ultimate truths or standards, just copies of cultural copies; no original anything.

From a biological perspective, *nothing gets abstracted creating* **the illusion of an external world**. Hence the world and "I" are simulations; a copy of a copy with no original. If Quantum Physics is correct, then everything is in constant flux as atoms exchanging with other atoms to form different substances; i.e., copies of copies with no original. Moreover, what we call "now" or "the present" is always deferred because it is relational to past and future, and time itself is an abstraction, a linguistic construction which is perceived dependent, hence, there is no beginning and no original.

Sutra li: The world is a simulation of nothing!!! There are no simulations.

Commentary

From not only a physics and biological, but also a Buddhist perspective, there is no separate, individual, independent thing. No-_thing_ is not nothing as in the sense of a thing, but as "**is not**." Why? Because no separate individual thing exists, and because even the perceive**r** or "I" which "sees" the void **is not**; the "I" is a condensation of the no<u>thing</u>ness (physics) or a coming together of chemicals which produces the _perceiver-I_, after the action or event has already occurred (biological), or a condensation of consciousness (Advaita/Tantra). _The nervous system, through abstracting, omitting and selecting out produces the illusion of a solid world with separate independent individual objects that appear to be independent of one another; from all approaches, this is non-existent._

Moreover, the nervous system using instruments such as microscopes now "sees" and _infers_ molecules, atoms, etc, and their movement; hence the "I's" postulation of things which change, have energy or mass. All this is *information* and is made available only through the vehicle of the nervous system with its abstracted *perceiver-I* through the process of abstraction-representation. This means that the perceivables as well as the perceiver appear and disappear only through perception.

Therefore all simulations have no origin and without a nervous system "are not." In this way, everything is a hyper-real fabricated reality based on nothing.

> **Buddha in the Diamond Sutra said it this way, "There is no world."**

Sutra lii: Everything you see is a memory.

Commentary

*T*he perceiver arises after the action or event has already occurred. If memory is defined as something that has already occurred, this means that what you see is a memory. Memory is a sensory abstracted map made of nothing. Therefore what you see is an abstracted map which appears as something, but is not there.

Sutra liii: Models and Spiritual systems are simulations of Nothing.

Commentary

Models are abstracted representations of nothing as is the *subject-I* and the physical world that the *perceiver-I* perceives.

Nothing is real, since representations are not representations of *some*thing. Rather, they are abstractions of **nothing**, and as such, are models without an original.

Spiritual or psychological philosophy therefore is a system of words based on abstracted representations of **nothing**, with no origin, source, or center.

The world is devoid of meaning outside of an abstracted language system; it is a universe of theories floating in a void.

For post-deconstruction, this is not bad. On the contrary, in the book, *Quantum Consciousness* (pg.173 and 176 ,1993), you can notice a similar understanding of concepts floating in the void. It is critical for both Buddhism and Advaita-Vedanta that these concepts are made of nothingness, in other words their appearance is perceiver-dependent. This *recognition* brings nirvana as extinction.

There are several different ways to understand what could be termed a crisis in spiritual realization—*simulation*, and what Baudrillard calls the *hyper-real*.

Simulation: a copy of a copy for which there is no original. Understanding this means that what we see is an abstraction, a copy. For example, if I look at this **book**, and then close my eyes, I see an image of the **book** I was looking at which is a copy of the **book**. The "original" **book** is an abstraction of the nervous system and represents an estimated .000054% of the stimuli that was that "original" **book** you were looking at. Actually **there is no original book**. What you see or imagine is a *simulation* and there is no original, only a representation of an original which is actually made of nothing. Think about it this way. Prior to the nervous system, there is **The Substance**. On a Quantum level, there are atomic particles which are constantly changing. The nervous system through omission *constructs* a **book** map. The **book** is an abstraction, a representation which has *no original*. Why? Because the constant change at the atomic level can not be seen. "You never put your foot in the same river twice" (Heraclitis). "You never put your foot in the same river once" (Clatitius). Hence, there is no original **book** of **books**. There is no origin of anything, only representations of representations of representations of representations.

> *This brings us to Nisargadatta Maharaj who is parroted in Post-deconstruction's "**Nothing exists**." This translates as there is no original source or presence from which what you see or perceive was derived.*

Because of *simulation,* in psycho-spiritual circles we see what Baudrillard calls the *hyper-real.* **The model that is taught and the behavior and experiences that are expected (either in psychotherapy or spirituality) become more real than the actual experienced reality than it supposedly represents.** The *hyper-real* is a model without origin or reality.

Today in hyper-real simulations of spiritual circles, in order for things to be considered real, they have to be more real than real itself, or hyper-real. The illusion has taken hold on a spiritual level with more enlightened masters than ever. Workshop presenters and gurus become hyper-real, not real. Hence, they all look alike in white or orange, sitting on a throne, creating hyper-real images which we expect, demand and buy. Look at your most prominent gurus and workshop leaders.

"Smoke and mirrors," they say, suggesting "You can have it all" and *"the sizzle becomes more important than the steak,"* the story more important than the reality. For example, how many people do you know who are any happier, more fulfilled or enlightened, even after 10, 20, 30 years of spiritual or psychological practice? The model or hyper-real has become more real than the human experience. The spiritual seeker and client in psychotherapy has become the new consumer or new customer. Spiritual customers or consumers put down consumption of material goods and replace it with the *consumption of ideas, spirituality and mythologies posing as reality.*

We have taken the simulation as real. How does that effect us in the area of psychology and spirituality? We expect instant therapeutic success to be like fast food, and call it brief therapy or instant enlightenment. We assume the presentation (the act) is real, buffered by spiritual props of thrones, orange, all white or purple cloth and someone saying mantras such as *be present,* or *the presence,* holding their hands and smiling in the namaste or prayer position. Soon the simulation, the look, is what becomes important and the underlying feelings beneath them are not important.

This tendency of gurus, therapists, new age teachers, philosophies and value systems can be called "**kitsch.**" **Kitsch** is a German word born in the middle of the sentimental 19th century. Repeated use, however, has obliterated its original metaphysical meaning. **Kitsch** is the absolute denial of shit, in both the literal and the figurative sense of the word. **Kitsch** excludes everything from its purview which is essentially "unacceptable in human existence" (The Unbearable Lightness of Being).

Kitsch tends to simplify complicated ideas and thoughts into stereotypical and easily marketable forms. **Kitsch** appeals to the masses and to the lowest common denominator. It is the world of greeting-card poetry and velvet Elvis. For **kitsch** to be **kitsch**, it must evoke an emotional response "that the multitudes can share" (*Notes for Studies*, page 204).

Spirituality and psychology have become **kitsch**. We are no longer looking for a teacher who is human, who falls in and out of love, who might be married and divorced, who might lose money in the stock market, get angry or sick. We want the simulation. We want the guy in a white outfit, with a long beard, almost like Charleton Heston *in The Ten Commandments* with the big cane and white beard who speaks prophecy or remains in silence. We want the man who does good, thinks pure thoughts, looks happy and bright and always cheerful. These are the hyper-real **kitsch** gurus of spirituality that are accepted. A **kitsch** image has been created of more real than real, like God himself appearing in the flesh, on a throne, speaking words of wisdom. This is what people want in the simulation — more real than what is actually real, in short, *teachers who hide their shit*

Hucksters, gurus and workshop presenters are often times hyper-real and **kitsch**. They are bigger than life, full of energy, who profess they can create, have or manifest anything. **Kitsch** workshop presenters and **kitsch** gurus become hyper-real, not real. Hence they all look alike in white or orange sitting on a throne, and this is the image which is sold. The hyper-real knowledge or information peddlers sell their products called knowledge not for their value, but for the capital. Hyper-real **kitsch** seekers find this in line with a hyper-real **kitsch** value system: you can have it all.

One **kitsch** guru I knew decided that he had to clean up his *act*. He wasn't allowed to smoke cigarettes anymore. He shouldn't smoke marijuana anymore. If he used four letter words, they weren't translated. An image was created of more real than real, like God himself appearing in the flesh. This is what people want in the simulation, more real than what is actually real, in short, a **kitsch** guru, teacher, therapist or philosophy.

Words or *Signs*, according to Roland Barthes, is in everything from how we dress, move, act, comb our hair, speak or think.

Speech acts as a vehicle and sign of exchange. And, like all society, it is based on exchange, i.e., work for money or money for a car and even spiritual practice is exchanged for enlightenment.

The white bearded **kitsch** teacher dressed in white who teaches or remains in silence is constantly producing *non-verbal signs or giving non verbal signals* in this case as second level of communication. "I am enlightened," is a sign, a cliché of the enlightened master. This is why in the movie the *Ten Commandments*, Moses (Charlton Heston) wears a white outfit with long white hair and a white beard. These are the society and culture signs which signal one who is enlightened

In the hyper-real world, words no longer mean anything in everything from the political, e.g., George Bush's, "war is peace," to psychology's reframing (spining) pain as an opportunity for growth, or as a lesson coming from "somewhere" or some logo-centric god to the new wave of self-appointed **kitsch** gurus claiming and promising enlightenment.

Be more, do more, have (consume) more.
That is the definition in the new hyper-real
kitsch psychology and spirituality.

Sutra liv:: If there is no self, then there is no Spirituality, all spirituality is I-dependent.

Commentary

What is a self? Is there a self at all? What is spirituality? To best grasp this, let us look in the following directions.

Biological. If "I" and what the "I" perceives are both abstractions of nothing, then there is no self and without a self there is no spirituality.

Physics. If what we call the body and the "I" are composed of subatomic particles floating in space, how can we even consider that we have will, volition or choice, or that we exist as a separate entity let alone that we may have a psychological or spiritual process because at the subatomic level there is no separate, independent, individual "I."

Advaita-Vedanta/Hindu Yoga/Tantric Yoga. If there is only one interconnected substance, call it consciousness or Brahman, and we are made of that same substance, and there is no individual self with volition or will, how can there be a spirituality?, and for whom is there to be spirituality?

Hindu Yoga. If everything including the "self" or "I" is made of and subject to the play of the elements and forces, then there is *no-I* and no individual self that can claim doership or ownership of a spiritual life.

Quantum Psychology. If all that is perceived or conceived including the perceiver is a representation of nothing, *then the perceiver as well as the perception of nothing is also "not."*

In addition, If everything perceivable is an abstraction of nothing, and the "I" and spirituality and psychology are abstractions of nothing and exist in language only, then the "I" and spirituality are linguistic manifestation.

Spiritual and psychological theories are made of nothing and float in nothing.

Sutra lv: There is no reality.

Commentary

There can be no reality since everything perceivable or conceivable is a representation and not a representation *of* something. Rather, they are abstractions of nothing, but not as a representation *of* something, and as such, are models without an original.

Spiritual or psychological philosophy, therefore, is a system based on words which are representations of *nothing* with no existence, origin, source, or center.

Spiritual and psychological concepts as theories are abstractions and hence are devoid of an ultimate meaning or existence outside of the abstraction/ language process.

The universe is dependent upon the existence of a perceiver, a *subject-I* which is a fluid (bio-chemical) creation and an abstracted representation of nothing on a biological level. On a physics level, the perceiver or *subject-I* appears through the movement of sub-atomic particles that come together. For Advaita, the perceiver or *subject-I* is a manifestation of THAT ONE SUBSTANCE. Simply stated, *in order for the universe to exist, it requires a perceiver to perceive it.*

Sutra lvi: There is no sayer.

Commentary

As we can see, there is no doer because the action is done before the sense of "I" or doership arises. Moreover, there is no sayer. This means that there is no person "in there" who speaks. Actually, the words come out before an "I" is aware of what it says. *The "I" is past tense.* Words come out, and the "I"/sayer imagines it said it. Then the "I"/sayer takes credit, praise or blame for what was said, when the "I"/sayer appeared as part of the saying or sounds and words that have already come out.

Just remember how often "you" thought "you" said something or did something that you could not believe you said or did. Did you say or do it? The "I" comes with the words that are said and then the perceiver declares sayership. All sayers as well as doers are created after the saying or doing is over. In this way, all that is thought, said, done or perceived has already occurred before the "I" arises.

The "I" and perceiver arise after the writing and sound have already occurred.

Sutra lvii: *There is a great illusion that there is an entity, an "I," a self that hears, sees, knows, and cognizes.*

Commentary

To have a witness, a knower, an awarer requires two or more substances. However, if the knower and the known are one, then neither are. Moreover, Advaita-Vedanta suggests; THERE IS no HEARER, since THE HEARER AND THE SOUND ARE ONE.

There is no seer, since the seer and the seen are one. THERE IS NO SEER, THE EYE SEES.

There is no taster as the taster and the taste are one.

There is no feeler, as the feeler and the felt are one.

There is no knower as the knower and the known are one and hence are not.

Just as language gives the illusion by its nature, that there is a self speaking and an other listening, both are in words and are one.

The "I" is in language. All language is relational, therefore the "I" exists in language only (there is no I prior to the abstraction process and language). Within the context of language, the "I" can only exist in relation to other words and sounds. There can be no "I" outside of this linguistic relationship. Relationship in language and other words creates the "I." This means that even as Nagarjuna teaches dependent arising, even in language, there is no separate independent thing; all is dependent on all for its existence. Therefore, a separate, individual, independent self existence, even in language, is empty (is not).

Taking all these contexts into account, or as Nisargadatta Maharaj used to say, "And when I analyze all of this," you realize two pivotal things. First, there is no perceiver or perceived without a separate "I" to say the perceiver's perception even exists; two, the "I" or self does not exist as a separate independent entity and is therefore empty (Buddhism), and three, since the "I" or imagined self is an abstracted representation which has no existence outside of the abstraction/language process (biology-linquistics), then there is no perceiver or perceived, and hence, the perceiver and the perceived are empty, and are not. In this way, Buddhism negates itself, as does the neti-neti of Advaita Vedanta.

> This understanding destroys the
> illusion of being.

Sutra lviii: Consciousness is behind or underneath the illusion

Commentary

Consciousness provides **the great illusion of an existence prior to sound, words, or perception.** It is consciousness which makes perception and language appear to have a separate independent self nature, or existence.

This reminds me of my favorite Nisargadatta Maharaj story. When I was there, a French psychiatrist asked a very long-winded question about karma, reincarnation, births, deaths, credits, debits, merits, past lives and future lives, etc. Maharaj asked him, "Who told you that you exist?" After a long silence, Maharaj said, "Consciousness tells you that you exist and you believe it. If you understand just this, it is enough."

Sutra lix: There is no present-time.

Commentary

There is no present-time because there is no perceiver to perceive time until after the present has already passed. There is no time outside of a perceiver. Time is an abstracted representation of nothing. Time exists as a perception which is later reinforced by an abstracted language.

Rather than using the phrase "be here now," or "be in the present," better to call it no-time.

There is no past or future.

"The blink of the present instant is haunted from the start by the past and future" (G.G. Bennington). Each "moment of now" carries a trace-map of past and future. There is no "pure present," there is only a present with the trace of past and future. The present is a mark of the past and the future.

Sutra lx: The "I" carries with it the illusion of location.

Commentary

The power of voice which appears to comes out of this location called "I" when actually the sound of the voice and the perception of the voice arise at the same time as the *perceiver-I* and is heard after the sound has already occurred. The *perceiver-I* which arises after the sound is already made also appears as if it has a location, a sound center and origin, a "you" which speaks.

However, location occurs as a perceptual experience and the perceiver of speech is an abstraction, a coming together of fluids (biological), or condensed nothing (Buddhism – Physics – the Heart Sutra – Einstein). The location of speech, i.e., "It's coming from 'me' in this location," or "with 'me' as its originator" is an illusion, a perception, an experience, an abstraction only.

The illusion of an "I" as the originator of speech is an illusion based on a perceiver's perception "as if" the perceiver had a real existence and being and was not an abstraction (biology), a condensation of nothing (Quantum Physics), or form as emptiness (Buddhism or the Substance (Advaita-Vedanta).

The *perceiver-I* which hears this voice arises after the suppression of sounds which produces language and after the voice/sound has already occurred. The problem is that the voice's location and locator are imagined perceptions which appear after the sound is made.

It is quite extraordinary that as a composite of subatomic particles floating in space on a little rock called a planet within an insignificant solar system, we somehow not only imagine ourselves as important, but also as if we are a kind of a center with an actual location with the power of choice and separate individual independent ability to act independently of everything else.

Sutra lxi: The "I" exists as an abstraction in language only.

Commentary

*T*he "I" with its abstracted self-centered representational location, arises through biology which produces language. The "I" *illusions* an independent existence because the "I" splits-off or disconnects from sensation during the abstraction process "as if" it were separate from sensation. There is a disconnection between the movement from one level of abstraction (sensation) to the next level of abstraction ("I"). The "I" level of abstraction feels separate from the previous sensation level. The "I" level of abstraction imagines it is higher, the creator of the originator of sensation rather than it being an abstraction of the sensation level. The "I" level of abstraction assumes beingness which is imaginary. There is only "**dependent arising**" (**Nagarjuna**) and there is no "I" existing outside of abstraction/language.

Moreover, the "I" disappears upon investigation. To illustrate, ask yourself, "What is 'I'?" or look for "I" and notice that it disappears.

Language has a tendency to give the illusion of an existence prior to perception and outside of biology. For example, the illusion of a soul that exists in or out of space-time with a past, present, and future, with an independent, non-interrelational existence.

The "I" as an abstracted representation of nothing, cannot grasp its

1) non-independent origination (Buddhism),
2) arising through abstraction (biological),
3) impermanence (Buddhism),
4) dependent not independent self nature (Buddhism),
5) lack of presence or existence outside of language (Postmodernism).

Sutra lxii: The "I" and illusioned "other" is a representation of nothing.

Commentary

The "I" on a biological level is an abstraction, a representation of nothing. The "other" is also in language, as language is relational (in relation) to "other;" in this way both are abstractions of nothing.

For Saussaure, the "I" is a sign (word) whose sound is arbitrary, and for Wittgenstein words have meaning in language, how they are used, and by their differences to other words, i.e., "I" rather than "it."

The "I" is a word that has been patterned to signify a separate individual independent "self." "I" *therefore, is not "me." The "I" is a linguistic metaphor, as is "other" — an abstraction of nothing* whose meaning can never be determined because that can only be done in relation to other words which are also abstracted representations of nothing.

Sutra lxiii: There is no "I" that you are.

Commentary

There is no "I", no ego, no subject that stands in the world and thinks and confers something on what it sees and thinks. There is a language of thought, and *the "I" sound gives the illusion of a formal point of reference or location for it.*

In Quantum Psychology we would say that there is no thinker, *the thinker and the thought are one and arise and subside together.*

The meaning of "I" has traces (tracks) of previous "I's." However, when asking, inquiring, or trying to get the answer to "Who am I?," we are left frustrated because the answer, *even silence, space or emptiness, is a non-verbal trace/track or representation. The perceivable blank or silence is still a perception to be discarded.* Hence, the answer to the question "Who am I?" can not be reached because the "I" is an arbitrary sound and any experience is an abstraction whose meaning is always already deferred. Moreover, "Who," "am" and "I" are words which are abstracted representations of nothing.

Let us use Roland Barthes (*The Death of the Author*) as an example. The sound R-O-L-A-N-D B-A-R-T-H-E-S is a sound which through language has come to mean this person who is different from other people. All personage or separation is in language only, as language and speech exist because of arbitrary customary differences. This sound through patterns forges the illusion of a proper name, a person, place or thing that exists. This illusion dissolves when we realize the person through the "I" sound exists as a linguistic representation only.

However, the name and sound R-o-l-a-n-d B-a-r-t-h-e-s is arbitrary, and as such its meaning is dependent upon how it is used. "Roland Barthes is great" means one thing. "Roland Barthes is an asshole" means something else.

The meaning of "Who am I?" or the "I" as a person "is not" because the meaning of "who you are" is always in language and as such is deferred and an abstraction of the nervous system produced by sensation which is prior to the "I" sound and hence prior to what you call a "you."

Shiva Sutras: All bondage is caused by sound.

When asked "Who are you?," Nisargadatta Maharaj answered, *"Nothing perceivable or conceivable."*

Sutra lxiv: There is no substance that exists prior to the word substance.

The word and sound substance is a sound an abstraction, a linquistic metaphor, which does not exist outside of the abstraction/language process. The word substance as an abstracted representation stands in for something which does not exist, without an "I" or perceiver there to perceive it.

Sutra lxv: The "I" was thrown into the world.

Commentary

Martin Heidegger's brilliant existential statement is that we are *thrown into the world*. This concept of being *thrown into the world* is the origin of what we call psychology because biologically through the movement of fluids, the "I" literally finds itself here. The "I" did not choose to be in this world. The "I" did not decide to come here, the "I" appeared not by its own volition or will. The "I," the sense of beingness, was **thrown into the world** from where the "I" can only fantasize or spiritualize (God, a soul, another plane, to learn lessons, to pay off some karma, etc.). The "I" cannot "know" since it is an abstraction of Nothing. The "I" then somehow imagines it created or had something to do with what is perceived.

A being, self or "I" is all of a sudden thrown in time and relates to the world as historical. The perceptual experience of being is actually a map, an abstracted representation of nothing which is produced by fluids. Therefore, the *illusion of being* must be deconstructed or at least confronted in order to realize who you were prior to this *map of being*.

The problem with psychology is that it strives to analyze this being, "I" or self which was **thrown into the world,** and then attempts to change a self or make it better by comparing it to societal standards. **Post-deconstruction would call this "a mirage which is trying to make a better mirage."**

Analysis leads the self further from itself, as the nervous system produces more and more abstractions about who or what it is was or how or why it is here. You could say that it gets further away from itself as it theorizes its existence. This self, this being, must be extinguished. Otherwise, the self always determines itself by abstractions.

The "I" is trying to deal with its "thrownness," not *realizing* that *it just appeared.* The "I" assumes that there must be a creator. The falsity lies in the fact that the "I" did just appear, and that the "I" *was* thrown into the world. *The sense of "I" appears through a chemical reaction in the brain.* We assume that we were created. How else could we have gotten here? That leads to our problems. Therefore, everything that is revealed, understood, perceived or experienced by the *I am* is more false than the *I am* itself. There is a basic assumption that "*I am,*" and that there is a world.

Sutra lxvi: *There is no volition.*

Commentary

If the "I" is an abstraction, produced by chemicals in the brain and arises after the event or action has already occurred, then the idea of volition and no doership is an illusion produced by the nervous system. How does the illusion of volition and choice illusion us? To illustrate, an "I" perceives that *"I am"* sitting here at my desk and all of a sudden "I" say to myself, "'I' will now lift my arm," and "I" lift my arm or "'I' will now stand up," and "I" stand up. Why is that not volition and choice? Why am "I" not the doer or chooser? Why don't "I" have the volition to raise my hand? Why don't "I" have will?

The answer can be derived through the work of noted philospher, David Hume (*circa* 1750). What David Hume said is that all experience is mediated by the nervous system and everything that we experience is not the thing itself, but rather a representation of the thing. Therefore, saying, "I am now going to raise my hand," or, "I am now going to stand up", **illustrates the idea of volition and will, and that doership is an abstraction and representation that occurs through the act of self-perception. Self-perception occurs after the action or event takes place through the abstraction process.** Since all acts of perception are representations and abstractions which are perceived after they occur, they are not accurate and they are not what is. Since **the nervous system is late**, when we see something, we see an abstracted or solidified representation of what has already occurred. The 99.999% of the emptiness is left out. What we see and hear has already occurred and our conclusions or inferences are abstracted representations which occur after our abstracted perception. Therefore, the abstracted perception of volition, will, doership or choice is an assumption, an inference. Therefore, they are representations and abstractions and not what is. **All perceptions and experiences are an illusion of a nervous system** that omits 99.999%. The question to ask is **WHAT IS LEFT OUT?** *The answer is the emptiness.* It is mind blowing just to contemplate this point alone.

Sutra lxvii: There are no thoughts or motivation for speech.

Commentary

There is an illusion that there are reasons or motivations for speech, words and actions, in short a rationale. The "I," perceiver or say**er** of speech, do**er** of action or the reason**er** (the abstraction which comes up with the rationale or motivation for action) come after the action and after the words. This means that the assumptions or justifications for actions and speech are after the "I," perceives and as such are even greater abstractions (i.e., they omit even more).

Sutra lxviii-a: Dristi Shristi Vada, Sanskrit for, "the world is only there as long as there is an "I" there to perceive it."

Commentary

I first saw this simple yet powerful statement in the Yoga Vashistha, and it is worthy of the greatest praise and study. We will attempt to do it justice.

The nervous system abstracts from nothing automatically before the "I" and perceiver even appear. The "I" and the perceiver are abstractions formed biologically through the movement of bio-chemicals. From a physics perspective, the world is formed from the movement of subatomic particles which form atoms and molecules, all of which oc-curs as the abstracted perceiver or the I AM arises. The "I" is a linguistic metaphor, an abstraction, which exists as a representation of NOTHING. All sounds which produces abstractions called words are metaphors which mean that they stand-in for or represent things which can only be seen through an abstracted perceiver as produced through a nervous system but do not exist otherwise. If I say, "I saw a dog today," the word dog stands-in for an abstraction, which is the sub-atomic particles which the "I" perceives as a dog. I do not have to show you a dog. The word dog is a metaphor, an abstraction of nothing which is seen only through an abstracted perceiver. The dog does not exist without a nervous system there to produce an "I" and world to perceive it. Therefore, the world is only there if there is an "I" there to perceive it, or, as the Buddha said, "There is no world."

Sutra lxviii-b: "I am not the body." "There is no body." — Dristi Shristi Vada, Part ii

Commentary

This statement sits as a bastion of yoga, a major tenet which this sutra hopes to explain. First, the perceiver is an abstraction of nothing.

Second, what the nervous system perceives is an abstraction of an abstracted perceiver .

Third, the perception of a body, self or "I" is also an illusion produced through the abstracting process; the body is a perceivable and as such is an abstraction of nothing.

Fourth, rather than "I am Not the body," there is no body.

Fifth, since all perceivables are abstractions of nothing, the nervous system exists only as it is perceived by a nervous system's abstracting process.

Sutra lxix: 7here is no independent "pure" source or presence.

Commentary

It would be easy to jump to the conclusion that "I" am positing an origin, source or "intelligent" center by positing *the substance*.

However, though Advaita-Vedanta posits the one substance which they call Brahma, the substance does not exist unless there is a separate substance or illusioned witness to say it is so.

In Madhyamika Buddhism, no such source or origin is posited. Moreover, there is no binary, because if there is only *one substance*, all binaries vanish.

Post-deconstruction even more radically deconstructs the one substance which as a linguistic proposition exists as a sound patterned in language, as does the "I." Since both *the substance* and the *witness* are in language, neither have an abstracted pre-sound existence, an existence which exists prior to the abstraction process and later in language.

Moreover, if there was only *one substance,* there would be no "I" to know it. Nisargadatta Maharaj called this **unawareness,** prior to "I" which is the same as **Nirvana as extinction.**

Perceptions and linguistic terms such as "I" are metaphors which become a big illusioned continuous story that proves itself. Combining Wittgenstein theory leaves us with all propositions ("I's") as tautologies, *language games,* that prove themselves and whose function, use and existence are in language and perception only. Madhyamika Buddhism, like post-deconstruction, leads to no *thing,* a beyond that is not.

The question is, "Doesn't Advaita-Vedanta or Buddhism or Madhyamika Buddhism posit a center?"

No, Advaita-Vedanta says it is all *the substance,* understanding that there is no substance because there is no "I." Moreover, unlike most dualistic yogas and binary systems where one term, behavior, feeling, etc., is considered better or closer to God than another, neither Advaita-Vedanta nor Tantric Yoga posit such understanding.

Buddhism, in its doctrine of *impermanence,* does not posit a center. In its misunderstood interpretation, it does posit a binary system, i.e., compassion is better then passion, but in Madhyamika Buddhism, this is exploded and no binaries or center remains.

Sutra lxx: Find the space between two texts, called the discourse. This is Discourse "Seeing."

Commentary

Throughout Asia, the classic meditation instruction has been to find and stay in the space or silence between two thoughts or two breaths.

For Postmodernism, all languages are supplements and traces of other languages and texts *grafted* together to make a new text. For example, in our personal history, we might notice that we have "grafted," or in Quantum Psychology terminology, we "fused" with one part of another person (Identity). Throughout our lifetime, for survival, the nervous system grafted or fused together or took on various other people's identities to create a tapestry that we call "us" or "I."

However, the question still is and always was (since we are aware of and are not this grafting-fusing patchwork), "What or who am I?"

In the East, they ask us to notice the space or silence between two thoughts (texts or identities) and stay there. The same is true in Postmodernism. Derrida calls this space between two texts, the "hyman."

All of this subtly implies a self or *subject-I* that exists, has an existence prior to perception or words that is beyond the text(ual) or fused I-dentities. The subtly in Quantum Psychology was an attempt to demonstrate that the witness, observer, or awarer as "subject" was part of and was made of the same substance as what it was aware of. It is essential to include the witness, observer, awarer, or subject as the I-dentities or texts that are grafted together.

It must always be remembered that whatever the subject (by any name) is aware of, it is text-representation-abstraction, and that the awarer is also a representation-abstraction that must be discarded as not-this.

Moreover, the "subject" which witnesses or is aware of the space, silence or void between thoughts, texts, or structures, is also **NOT**, *since the witness and the witnessed are the same substance.* The subject deconstructs itself and samadhi (no-me) occurs spontaneously.

This "beyond" the "subject" deconstructs even the awarer of the void, or the one substance.

Sutra lxxi:. This realization moves us beyond and through the Yogic and Buddhist perspectives. In the Yogic and Buddhist perspectives, there are eight limbs, or folds.

Commentary

Yogas, both Hindu (Raja) and Buddhist, begin with the 8th-fold or 8-limb path. The 6th fold or limb is called Dharana (concentration practice), the 7th limb or fold is called meditation, and the 8th limb or fold, Samadhi. Beyond Samadhi could be called the 9th limb or fold. There is no "I" or step, fold or limb, where the no-"I" realization occurs. This is where the witness is "seen" as the same energy/consciousness as the witnessed. Nisargadatta Maharaj called this **unawareness, or Nisarga, the Natural Yoga.**

What becomes apparent after some time is that there is an "I" that "Oh so wants" to experience this **unawareness** or Nirvana. Obviously, this is impossible since there is no-I. This further clarifies that, *"You will not necessarily be aware of your own enlightenment"* (*Zen Master Dogen-Zenji, see Sutra xxxv*) or *"No being has ever entered Nirvana"* (Buddha).

Sutra lxxii: Discourse seeing locates the space between discourses.

Commentary

The discourse is both linguistic and phenomenological (contains experiences). The discourse "ventiloquises" us. The "I" arises as a suppression of sound, an abstraction of language, and as such the abstracted "I" echoes the discourse structures.

In this way, each sound is part of the discourse whether it be as simple as "I am bad," or as complex as Christianity or re-incarnation. There is no "I" separate from language, just a discourse that is so powerful and so pervasive as to appear as a "realistic" universe.

Wittgenstein called the process whereby we "see" one thing rather than another, *aspect seeing.* In his "rabbit/duck picture" (see illustration below), we can see only one at a time, the second one being omitted. Although not Wittgensteins' intention, this explains the way the nervous system sees things in binaries. It also explains how the term, in this case the visual image or experience, is omitted or "marginalized."

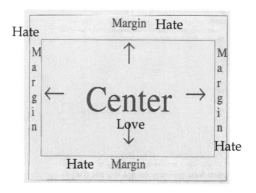

Declaring a localized center pushes its opposite to the margins.
De-construction is smashing a center and its margins.

Discourse seeing goes much farther in "seeing" not only the sensation(al) universe prior to discourse or from which the discourse is constructed, but also sees the "I," awar*e*r, perceiv*e*r, know*e*r of the discourse universe as part of the discourse universe.

Moreover, *discourse seeing* locates the space between discourses, even though it must be remembered that the space between the discourse along with its witness are both part of the discourse.

Sutra lxxiii: The space between discourse is an experience, and is therefore another discourse.

Commentary

*T*o have an experience, you must have a perceiver, experiencer, or a knower of the experience. All experiences are perceiver, experiencer, or knower dependent. The space between discourses is an experience, and therefore is just another discourse since space is a representation and does not exist separate from the space-discourse. Spiritual practice, or finding the space between, is a discourse which is a perception, an abstraction which includes perception and a perceiver and therefore is not.

Discourses appear at first as real and solid as your life. Upon realization, the discourse and "I" which exist as perceptions and in language only, appear more "sensation(al)" or "energetic." Prior to the discourse, the world appeared as a spiral, almost circular "energy pattern." Earlier, the energy pattern was floating in Nothingness beyond origin or source. With discursive dismembering through inquiry, ask: "What is the discourse?" It liberates one from the discourse beyond origin and source and the discourses' ventrilaquised "I." *Still there remains an awarer, until the **discourse of deconstruction is seen as discourse.***

Sutra lxxiv: The discourse of Spirituality occurs as an effect of the force of difference (difference with an "a").

Commentary

*A*ll spiritual practice requires a non-existent entity called "I" to do it. What follows are perceptual experiences of "I."

Spirituality is an effect of the force of difference (difference with an "a"). All spirituality is in words and perceptions which yield experiences. Spirituality appears through abstraction and only in relation to or how it refers to other words/experiences. All experiences, in this case spiritual experiences and philosophy, have meaning only in relation to other words, perceptions and experiences. The meanings of these experiences as "spiritual" are in words and perceptions as part of a spiritual discourse whose meaning and experiences are always in relation to other perceptions and other experiences.

Spirituality as a perception of "I" means that spirituality is a discourse that is a function and an effect of the force of differance (difference with an a). As such, it is an abstracted perceptual language game which you or an "I" can never get out of since the "I"-seeker-perceiver is part of the perceptual/spiritual/abstracted/experiential discourse.

Sutra lxxv: All models, structures and philosophy are produced to organize and handle chaos.

Commentary

*T*he production and organization of psychological structures by the nervous system are an abstraction, a metaphor to organize and handle chaos. Chaos, in this sense can also mean the way perception, experiences and meaning are always, deferred, as in relating to other words.

One must bear in mind that language and *language games* only prove themselves through the vehicle of language. They prove nothing and say nothing outside of the system of discourse that is being used.

Language games are a tautology that represent things which have no existence outside of or prior to the abstraction/language process.

The *language game* called Truth with a capital *T* is an abstracted linguistic metaphor filled with anthropomorphic truths that are true only within that specific *language game*. Once **the truth** *language game* is seen as a linguistic illusion, the **truth language game dissolves** since it no longer holds any interest or value.

Spirituality and psychology are only significant within the context of the *language game* of psychology or spirituality. Both are interesting at best, but inherently contain no chance of reaching fulfillment or meaning within them.

Sutra lxxvi: The Self is created through the suppression of the realization of differance (difference with an "a").

"The self is a suppression of differences."
— Derrida

Commentary

In *post-deconstruction,* the self exists as an abstraction and later in language only. The self is a by-product of the abstraction/language process.

The context of language, no-self or agency can best be translated as: all language is the structure of speech. Speech, as an abstraction of language, carries with it the suppression of differences in sounds and words which promote, produce or support what can or could be constructed as a self or an "I" which arises after the action, event, speech or perception has already occurred (biology). *This imaginary abstracted self* imagines agency or doership after the action or event has already occurred (Advaita-Vedanta).

The suppression of the realization of the absence of self is contained within the suppression of language as a linquistic pattern which forms this self. This no self or absence of self must be suppressed in order for a self to appear.

This aligns itself with the abstraction and constancy principles of biology (see *Sutra lxxvii* below) and is echoed by Buddhism which declares there is no self nature or independent origination, or as Derrida might say, "The 'I' is a supplement to the text; therefore the 'I' is a part or supplement of *no-I*."

Sutra lxxvii: The nervous system omits or suppresses the constant changes (differences) in perceptions and experiences, thus giving the illusion of a permanent changeless self.

Commentary

The biological aspect of *constancy* can be described as the nervous system's ability to omit or suppress constant changes (differences). The change might include anything from an awareness of the constant death and birth of cells, circulation of blood, movement of food, to the production of a **constant steady solid illusionary perception which produces the illusion of a solid body.** This self, too, is habitually formed through the suppression-(omission)-abstraction of ongoing biological and environmental changes, fabricating a self and a solid, stable world. It is the habitual use of neurological pathways that keeps the world and our perceiver of the world with the illusion of permanency or constancy constant. *This illusion of* *permanency veils a major tenet in Buddhism: "Everything is impermanent."*

Sutra lxxviii: There are no things that words represent.

Commentary

Since all words are abstracted representations of nothing, then words represent non-existent things.

All signifiers (words) are only referrals to other words which have meaning only in relation to other words within an abstracted linguistic system, therefore, there can be no referreds or signifieds, or things that actually exist outside of words.

Each word is always referred and deferred, and as an abstraction of nothing has no separate, individual, independent existence. Therefore, there is no origin or original in words, and hence no beginning in time, only a deferred time which exists in words with no beginning or origin.

When you speak to yourself, the illusion is that there is a self talking and a self listening. The illusion is there are two, i.e., the addressee and the addressor. There is a rupture between the addressor (self) and the addressee which dissolves when they are apperceived as one.

Sutra lxxix: The perception of an other "out there" is an abstracted representation.

Commentary

The "I" is an abstracted representation, so too is the linguistic "other." Both appear in language as if they were separate, rather than as an on-going sentence laced with the illusion of a speaker and a "spoken to."

Sutra: lxxx: "Nothing exists at any time or place having arisen by itself, from another, or from either.
— Nagarjuna's 2ⁿᵈ century Madhyamika Buddhism

Commentary

Nagarjuna called this *dependent arising*. Since everything has dependently arisen, then everything is unceasing, unborn, and without a separate, individual, independent self-nature. This is and moves us toward impermanence—

- not coming, not going
- without distinction, (differences)
- without identity, (sameness)
- free from conceptual construction

The Eight Negations of the "Middle Path" by Nagarjuna further explain the Middle Path expounded by Shakyamuni Buddha's Teaching.

Each thing exists only in virtue of its opposite. Therefore, all things are relative, without an individual, separate, independent permanent self-nature and are therefore empty (sunyata) of separate, individual, independent existence. The existence of any one thing must include the existence of other things.

We can easily see this as we look at sub-atomic particles, each non-permanent and ever changing without an existence separate from any other particle, or the perceiver (organizer of it). As mentioned in our earlier discussion of language and words, no word can exist separately or can act independently of other words. In order to exist in a language system, each word is dependent and refers to other words in order to derive its meaning.

Opposites are mutually dependent, therefore independent, separate, individual entities can not exist. Moreover, since everything is made of the same substance, everything is empty of a separate, individual, independent existence. Emptiness means the absence of a separate, individual, independent, permanent existence, not their non-existence as a phenomena; just their dependent arising.

Eight Negations of Nagarjuna
(describe the way it is not)
1. No creation; are not born
2. No elimination; they do not die
3. No destruction; they do not cease to be
4. No eternity; are not eternal

5. No unity; nothing is the same as anything else
6. No manifoldness; nothing is different from anything else
7. No arriving; they do not come
8. No departing; do not go

The Eight Negations of Nagarjuna As Four Pairs

- neither birth nor death (perishing nor arising in time)

- neither ending (impermanent) nor permanence (eternal)

- neither self-identical (the same) nor different

- neither coming nor going

It is by directly seeing that everything is dependently originated that we can understand that everything is empty of inherent, independent, individual, separate self existence. There is no "I," self, subject or soul.

Sutra lxxxi: The Buddha is without a self-existent nature; the cosmos is also without a self-existent nature.

Commentary

*N*ot only does an "I" not exist, the substance (Advaita) and Buddha Nature do not exist either. Nor are there teachings or a teacher to teach them._

> "No Dharma anywhere has been taught by the Buddha."
> — Nagarjuna

Sutra lxxxii: Spirituality as language is only one movement of difference (difference with an a).

Commentary

*A*ll language is made of the substance. All language traces or provides a face for the substance. All traces and faces are the substance, prior to the trace or face. *There is only the substance.*

This can be likened to the understanding that can be gotten from the Zen **Koan of koans:** *show me your original face.* This no face, no "I," all faces (substance), no face, is the answer to this koan; there is no face or "I."

Sutra lxxxiii: Nagarjuna's sunyata (devoidness of being or self-existence) is absolute negation.

Commentary

That no one is self-existent is the meaning of Sunyata.

That there is no self prior to the abstraction/word process is Sunyata.

*N*ararjuna is one of the few who goes beyond presence or origin and deconstructs theology, philosophy, language, gods and a pre-existent self-presence. He emphasizes **dependent arising as the essence of the emptiness of any separate independent being.**

Quantum Psychology states there is
no presence or origin prior to the
abstraction process which produces
through fluids a perceiver
and an experience.

Sutra lxxxiv: 7here is no "is" that is.

Commentary

hat is, is. This common expression in today's *pseudo Zen world* of the human potential movement provides the belief that there is an "is," a presence which actually is. **There is no "is" or presence** prior to an abstracted perceiver or an experiencer.

The word "is" is a representation, a description, a linguistic metaphor, an abstraction, "as if" something *is*.

• Understanding via Buddhism, there is no separate individual self that exists.

- Understanding through postmodernism, there is no identity, self-identity or presence which is carried into a "present-time" outside of language.

- Understanding through biology, "is" is a word, perception, an experience and as such is an abstraction of the nervous system.

- Understanding through <u>Advaita-Vedanta</u>, there is only one substance, and there is no "is."

It is the assumption that "is" exists which underscores and begins the search for meaning in all philosophies and religions. The "is," the "now," the present, or existence is a word or sign which points to another word or sign which points to another word or sign *ad infinitum*, whose meaning is always already deferred and is dependent upon the past and future. Hence, the Buddha says, "There is no self (independent) nature." We would add, "There is no self, presence or (independent) nature" outside of an abstracted representational linguistic system."

Sutra lxxxv: The "I" is not "I."

Commentary

This statement lies at the core of both Advaita-Vedanta and what the Buddha said.

In Advaita-Vedanta, there is no "I," only one substance. If we go with what the Buddha directly said, *there is no separate individual self.* In general semantics, *"I am" is not" I am"* because the "I am" changes each moment as does the sub-atomic level, even though the perceiver can not perceive it. In Post-deconstructionism, and according to David Hume, Because of the delay in how the nervous system works, the self only sees what has already occurred.

Sutra lxxxvi: The void is not.

Commentary

The void is oftentimes mistakenly perceived or witnessed by Buddhists as a center or source representing a whole. The void, or rather the perception of the void, is still a perception and as such is nervous system based. Moreover, the void is a representation. Ultimately, the void voids itself and hence there is no center or void as source or logos which exists. In Madhaymika Buddhism, post-deconstruction or what the Buddha directly said, , there is no *thing*. Madhyamika Buddhism voids the void experience. As the Dalai Lama said, "The mind is devoid of mind." This is as definitive a statement as "Everything is consciousness; nothing exists outside of consciousness." If everything is consciousness, even the knower of consciousness is consciousness; then there is no consciousness since there is no-I to identify it as such.

Sutra lxxxvii: There is no "I" separate from fluids.

Commentary

From a bio-chemical perspective, there is no "us." There are chemicals such as carbon, oxygen, hydrogen, phosphorus and nitrogen, which form genetic materials. From a neuro-science point of view, these materials form what we call an "I" which is made of fluids in the brain called neuro-transmitters which carry with them the "I" and the information the "I" has about itself.

"Fluids come together and all of a sudden, you think that you are."
— **Nisargadatta Maharaj**

Sutra lxxxviii: Samadhi is a state of nothing—no me.

Commentary

Samadhi is nothing. You only infer Samadhi when you are *not* in Samadhi. Samadhi is a state of nothing. In order to appreciate this, let us look at all Buddhist and Hindu yogas, which are called 8 limbed, and could very very loosely be described as 8 steps. To simply state, Limb 6 is called Dharana, or concentration practice: "The ability to rest the mind on an object without strain or going out of control" (*The Encyclopedia of Eastern Philosophy and Religion*, pg. 285). This leads to Limb 7 which in Raja Yoga is called dhyana or meditation: "The mind no longer projects its own concepts onto the object of meditation, instead merges with the object iself" (ibid), which leads to Step 8 in Raja yoga, called Samadhi: "In which duality and the manifest world no longer exist"(ibid). This takes us beyond Limb 8 or Samadhi and beyond yoga itself to *no-I* realization when the witness is "seen/ experienced" as the same energy or consciousness as the witnessed itself.

Sutra lxxxix: Words and experiences give the illusion of presence (an existence prior to the abstraction process).

Commentary

Once the thing that a word represents is believed to have an actual existence prior to words, a centering or logos occurs whereby as a center, the absence or emptiness becomes marginalized. We then inquire, "What is left out?" "What is being suppressed?" "What is being marginalized?" "What has been excluded?" Each of these, when asked in a repetitive manner, first reveals what had been suppressed or marginalized, and then the "substance."

Emptiness
Form (Center)

Form
Emptiness (Center)

Sutra xc: There is no present time.

Commentary

" **C**onsider the flight of an arrow. If reality is what is present at any given instant, the arrow produces a paradox. At any given moment, it is in a particular spot and never in motion. However the arrow is in motion from the very beginning to the end of its flight, yet its motion is never present at any moment of presence. The arrow's motion is always marked with the traces of past and future. Motion can be present only if the present instant is not something given but a product of relations between past and future." (*Deconstruction*, by Cullen, pg. 94).

From a Buddhist perspective, there can be no self or presence because self and presence insist upon independence and permanence, a self separate from another self, object or event. Since there is only "*dependent origination*" and *impermanence*, there is no separate self, and no separate presence.

More importantly, since *the I arises after the event or action occurs, then you can never perceive or experience "now."*

$\mathfrak{S}$utra xci-a: 7here is no cause and effect.

"A crow alights on the coconut palm tree and at about that very moment, a ripe coconut falls. The two unrelated events seem to be causally related in time and space, though there is no causal relationship."

**The Supreme Yoga,
by Swami Venkateshananda**

Commentary

can not over-emphasize the importance of dropping the *cause-effect illusion.* The best way I transmitted this experience was in the first exercise of the first meditation class in 1982 which became the jumping off point for Quantum Psychology. *Focus your attention on the experience rather than the object of experience.* In other words, unfuse the story as to why you feel what you feel and focus on the feelings themselves as consciousness. This unfusing drops the illusion that what someone said or did has something to do with what I am feeling, thus dismantling *the illusion of a space-time event causing an experience.* This is explained in the quote above as a crow alights on a coconut tree *and at about the same moment...*

Another way to appreciate this is to break down cause and effect. As everything is one substance and inter-connected, **the effect is the cause.** Let's imagine you get angry with me. I ask you, "Why are you angry?" You say, "Be-cause you said 'X'." "X" is then determined to be the cause and the effect is anger. I then say, "Well, I said 'X', be-cause my friend hurt my feelings." Now my friend who hurt my feelings is the cause and what I said to you was the effect. But why did my friend hurt my feelings? It was be-cause his wife divorced him. Now the wife becomes the cause and his hurting my feelings becomes the effect. Obviously, this could go *on ad infinitum;* hence, there is no specific local individual cause and effect.

Cause, or to imagine a cause, is to decide an endpoint as the cause.

To illustrate:

"I" go for a job interview and "I" believe that "I don't deserve to get the job." And it happens that I don't get the job. I decide to go to a therapist whose map says, "Ah, childhood-mom-dad," and through therapy it is determined that the cause of my belief, "I don't deserve it" is from my parents. Therapy creates a *territorialized* cause—mom and dad. In other words, out of all the possibilities in the universe, a small enclosed (artificial) territory of family is decided to be the cause and the effect of my belief "I don't deserve," and hence, "no job.

In order to deconstruct, dismantle or deterritorialize this, we must first notice that "no job" is the *effect,* and the *cause* is my family. But what caused my family to produce this belief? DNA might be one cause of my family belief, "I don't deserve it" which means my family's belief is the effect of the DNA. So the cause "family" is actually the effect. We then say, "What caused the DNA to replicate this structure?" The biochemistry prior to the DNA is the cause, and the DNA is the effect. What caused the biochemistry to react this way? The molecules of oxygen, hydrogen, nitrogen, potassium, etc., forced this to occur. So the *cause* of the biochemistry is the way oxygen, hydrogen, etc., moved or came together and that is the *real* cause of my not getting the job.

The problem we face in trying to terrritorialize a cause is that we separate, isolate and presuppose a separate independent subject, entity or element, and hence lose the substance. "Everything depends upon everything else" (Nagarjuana).

By using the family to territorialize, psychology creates the illusion of a separate, independent, individual event; so too does all science and spirituality when they presuppose a cause and effect relationship based on an independent subject, entity, element or subatomic particle that somehow caused the present situation under the overriding term, "Karma."

As we have seen, causes and effects are deferred, or refer back endlessly to possible reasons or causes for events. The danger lies in enclosing or territorializing a cause which means freezing it in time and acting as if, "Ah! This is the cause." The habit of *causalizing* by freezing time might give the illusion of control. However, it is just that — an illusion. When causes are based on these illusions, it is no wonder why results are scanty in such endeavors as psychotherapy, and spirituality.

Motives, motivations, reasons and causes on a biological level are abstractions which arise after the action or event has occurred. The concern with this, as far as understanding the process, is that the nervous system seeks causes by first beginning with the perceived effects, and then determining their cause. Also, the nervous system attributes motivations (sometimes good intentions, sometimes bad) to actions and events that have already occurred. Hence, justifying, explaining and creating reasons and maps that explain actions for which *the "I" was not even present.* To best illustrate, let us imagine again the situation of the person who did not receive the job who believed that was be-cause, "I didn't deserve it." The alleged motivation of setting oneself up for failure or proving the belief is true, is an abstraction. An assumption placed there by a *subject-I*, which occurred after the event through the coming together of fluids in the brain.

How can assumptions that yield motivations even be considered plausible? And yet, there is an industry of psychology based on an abstracted *subject-I* that further abstracts its motivations for an action which occurred before "the I" even arose, and later abstracts a "healthy" or "unhealthy" label based on these abstracted definitions.

In short, life happens, and after it happens, an abstracted *subject-I* arises to explain, justify or understand why it did.

Since everything is dependent on everything, with no independent arising, then there is no cause. Causes are always deferred. Every effect relates back to another cause that is an effect; therefore, we can never get to the cause.

And therefore we can never get to the effect.Since there is only one substance, and the cause and effect are one, then there are no causes and no effects. All imagined causes are abstractions, perceptions, thoughts, concepts or ideas of causes, and as such, are illusions of the nervous system's abstraction process.

How can a concept prove or validate another abstracted concept? *Since the substance, the cause and the effect are one, the substance is the cause and the effect as well.*

Sutra xci-b: *"Since things are dependent and dependent arising, then there can be no cause and effect." — Nagarjuna*

Commentary

Since everything arises and is dependent upon all other things (dependently originated or arising), then independent, separate, individual "things" do not exist by themselves. Dependent origination means that all things are empty of separate, independent, individual self-existence. Therefore, since there is no independent existence, causes, effects, and causality are **empty** of separate independent existence or a separate independent self-nature. All of these should be seen as illusions. Dependent origination leads to the emptiness of all things as separate entities.

> *No cause and effect is*
> *"The Law of Nothingness."*
> **— Nagarjuna**

Sutra xcii: All knowledge or information of causes is dependent upon the information you were given, i.e., the Siva Sutra, "Knowledge is bondage."

Commentary

*P*art of learning, in particular learning a language includes learning how to make casual connections. Learning a language is learning to name things and how they can be used "as if" they and the user were separate entities. Since at first this seems obvious, so what? Much of what we learn about how things are linked and caused is through culture. To illustrate, let's go back a few hundred years. Many people facing illness were bled as a cure for disease be-cause it was believed that the reason for an illness was bad blood which needed to be bled out. In many cultures, even today when there is drought, some believe the cause is that God or some form of God is angry. For this reason, priests are hired to chant mantras or to do certain rituals like offering flowers to rectify the situation. Many people believe that it is be-cause God is teaching them a lesson and that is the cause for their illness, and if they can learn their lesson, the illness will vanish. Giving up cause-effect relationships is difficult be-cause it is culturally ingrained, but making it even more difficult is that it is linguistically ingrained as well. Even more difficult, on a psychological level, believing we have found the cause gives us a feeling of control — if somehow we can control the cause, then somehow we can control the effect (outcome).

To attribute causation would require a set of discrete, separate, independent entities, which is incompatible with not only a Buddhist and Advaita approach, but also a physics, biological, and tantric understanding.

Sutra xciii: *The "I" appears as a response to a stimulus.*

Commentary

*T*he "I" along with its perceptions arises after the action and event has occurred, and with the "I" arises the illusion of beingness, and the grander illusion of volition and choice.

The *Shiva Sutra says that sound is the cause of bondage.* It is sound that is trance-duced by the brain producing sound images, and the illusion that the hearer is separate from the heard.

This sound produces the illusion of a stimulus and a response, or an "I" which responds to a stimulus.

Actually, *the "I" you call "you" is the response to a stimulus!!!* There actually is no "I" separate from the response or responder. Rather, it is the *response-I* (not an "I" which responds) that is produced anew containing the illusion of space-time location and beingness. But the *response-I* appears later or after the action or event has occurred.

Sutra xciv: Neurologically, the effect occurs before the cause, and the effect determines the cause.

Commentary

Although this is redundant, it is more than important that this be hammered home, because this delusive tendency to imagine a cause when actually the cause comes after the effect is so strong. This imagining a cause must be and can be exposed for what it is—an illusion!!!

On the level of neuroscience, first there are sensations, then after a while, a perceiver arises as an abstraction of the sensations. After a time, the perceiver labels the sensations as a feeling like anger, love, etc., then after a while the perceiver looks to find an "external" cause for the sensations which were labeled as a feeling (anger, love, etc.). This means that the effect called labeled sensations occurred prior to the illusioned cause, the externally perceived event.

To illustrate. You are sitting with someone with whom you have a close relationship. That person makes a remark which hurts your feelings. Most people would mistakenly assume that the remark caused the painful feelings. The remark in this story is the illusioned cause, the feelings are the effect. Let's analyze this. First, there are the sensations; after a while, through the abstracting process, the nervous system produces a perceiver. After a while, the perceiver notices the sensations and labels them as "hurt." After a while, the perceiver, looking for a cause, assumes it was the "external" remark that caused the hurt. As you can see, the effect (labeled sensations) called "hurt" occurred before the imagined cause called "the other person's remark."

It cannot be overstated that we all must get over the habit of attributing a cause.

The world is built upside down. On a nervous system's abstraction level, sensation occurs before thought. First there is a sensation, then through abstraction, the *perceiver/I* appears, then the external cause. All of this takes place in time. That means that the *perceived* cause comes after the effect or labeled sensation. Thus, the cause is an effect of the labeled sensations, not the other way around.

> Take your attention off of the cause;
> focus on what is there as energy.

The Story of Karma

Much has been said about Karma and the Law of Cause and Effect. Karma does not mean cause and effect. Rather, Karma is the nervous system's attempt to organize chaos and to keep a constancy where there is actually a discontinuous abstracted story appearing out of Nothing.

Instead of saying, "It's my Karma," it's better to say, "It's my story."

What must be kept in mind is that everything and "I" mean _everything is an abstracted story_, whether it's the soul story, the death story, the psychological story or the spiritual story.

Moreover, the "I" is in the story or text, and there is no "you" outside of the story or text.

To illustrate even more dramatically, after publishing _You Are Not_, several friends came to me saying (and this is a composite), "Wow, you've written twelve non-fiction books."

My response was, and has always been, there are only fiction books, no matter what the book is, it is fiction; all language is an abstraction and as such is a metaphor. Therefore, _everything is fiction._

Derrida understood that all language is metaphor and all philosophy is "white mythology."

Sutra xcv: The stimulus and the response arise and subside together and are made of the same substance, Advaita and Tantric Yoga respectively.

Commentary

rom yet another approach, Advaita-Ve-danta, there is an illusion that first there is a stimulus and then a response. Actually, they occur together, and as the same substance. They are not.

Sutra xcvi: Bhaktis, Gnanis and all spiritual seekers desire permanent states, and permanent, pleasant feelings.

Commentary

Bhaktas are addicted to a feeling, be it a feeling of love or devotion, still it is a feeling. They chase around deities in the form of gurus and teachers in the hope of getting, absorbing or having a permanent feeling state, which they call love.

Gnanis are addicted to clarity, and discarding, uncovering and deconstructing in the hope of attaining something called a permanent state or no-state of something. For this they keep an "I" alive to "see," experience or witness what it is or will be like when nothing is there.

Spiritual seekers are desirous of experiences and preferably a permanent experience of "bliss," and want to get and have this pleasurable experience permanently.

> *"I am not in a state."*
> Nisargadatta Maharaj

Gurus' disciples seek and believe they are going to get the ultimate, pleasurable, permanent experience that will last forever; this idea some call "enlightenment."

> *"There is no such thing as enlightenment."*
> Nisargadatta Maharaj

ALL OF THIS MUST BE REALIZED AS THE ULTIMTE TRAP SO THAT THIS ADDICTIVE PLEASURE SEEKING TENDENCY WHICH MANY PEOPLE TERM SPIRITUALITY IS REALLY JUST PLEASURE SEEKING ENTERTAINMENT. MOREOVER, THE "I" CANNOT HAVE THIS EXPERIENCE BECAUSE IT REQUIRES NO "I." THERE IS NO-I THAT GETS ENLIGHTENED.

When a student said to Nisargadatta Maharaj, "I want to be happy," Maharaj replied, "That's nonsense; happiness is where the 'I' isn't."

Sutra xcvii: Desire does not cause suffering; it is the "I" sense arising with desire which produces the illusion of separation and suffering.

Commentary

*D*esire has been deemed and earmarked by the world of "spirituality" as a bad thing, somehow harmful, and always an obstacle on the path. Yet Postmodern philosopher, Gilles Deleuze, refers to *the body as a desiring machine.*

Post-deconstruction takes this one step further. **Desire is the life force.** Life happens and life is condensed to form desire which condenses further into everything from pleasure to power, from fame to money. Although this is not the place to go into it, in *The Way of the Human, Vol. I,* much time is spent going into separating biological needs like food, air, shelter, etc. from what become sublimated wants. All of these are not an indictment of desire, but rather, how experiences which are abstractions territorialize desire which then yields pain.

The Buddha had Four Noble Truths. The **Second Noble Truth is**, "The cause of suffering is desire," and **the Third Noble Truth is**, "Elimination of desire ends suffering." For us, 2500 years after Buddha, there can be no disagreement, but rather a slightly, and I am sure agreeable shift in the understanding of the Four Noble Truths.

If there is only one substance which is life and nature itself which functions through desire, then it is not desire as the cause of suffering, but rather the territorialization and sublimation of desire seeking pleasure, name, fame, money, power, etc., as the cause of suffering.

If *desire is free floating energy*, then when there is desire with no *subject-I* which is made of free floating energy, then there is no suffering.

To illustrate, here is the ancient meditation from the Vijnanabhairava. "Focus your attention on the desire itself, rather than the object of desire." *This moves us from a Dharana (concentration practice), "limb" or "step "6 in Raja Yoga) through Samadhi and beyond to "step 9" no-"I" realization when the focuser too is "seen" as the same energy/ consciousness as* the desire itself. This de-territorializes the energy of desire and frees one from the habit of re-territorializing the free floating energy into a want in such a way as to bring pain and suffering. *More importantly, it moves one beyond concentration, meditation or even samadhi itself, since concentration and meditation both require an "I" to do them.*

Post-deconstruction states "the 'I' sense is formed with desire (as free floating energy) itself." Therefore, it is not that desire is bad or causes suffering, but rather **it is the "I" formation which arises simultaneously with desire that produces the illusion of suffering.** In this way and with this understanding, the culprit is the "I" which arises with the desire.

Free floating energy with no "I" forms desire with an "I," with a very specific, habitual way of fulfilling that desire. The *subject-I* occurs as the movement from pure life force (with no-subject-object separation) to desire with an "I" being formed (i.e., "I have a desire"), which then turns toward a desired object. When the abstracted *subject-I* feels the frustration of its territorialized "self" — imposed outlet, the "I" *later* abstracts reasons such as "There's a lesson," "God doesn't want me to have," "God is teaching me," "This desire takes my soul from God," etc.

It is the <u>*de-territorializing,*</u> also called in previous work *de-framing, no frames of reference, no references to frame* of the habitual which takes us back *prior to* the *subject-I.* As Ramana Maharishi said, "Go back the way you came."

All experiences are abstractions. As such, so is the search or desire for pleasure. Each pleasure as an experience is always deferred, or leaves us wanting or desiring more, better or different. This also includes the search and desire for spiritual experiences or even the ultimate spiritual experience called enlightenment.

Sutra xcviii: Pain is the desire to prolong pleasure and get rid of pain.

Commentary

What the "I" calls pleasure or pain is based upon the information and learning that has been passed down for generations. How often have we eaten and yet desired a little something else or think of a something else that would enhance the pleasure? Pleasure, except possibly at the moment of orgasm, is deferred and seeks difference (more, better, different).

This redefines Buddha's **Second Noble Truth**: *"All suffering is caused by desire."* Rather, all suffering is produced by

> *the attempt to avoid "pain" and prolong pleasure.*

Most of today's new-age spirituality wants and desires pleasurable feelings, i.e., *bliss*, which is labeled as spiritual, while also wanting to be rid of pain and hate, i.e., *piss*, which is labeled as unenlightened. Although Tantric yoga, Zen Buddhism, Advaita and Mahyamika Buddhism directly throw out these notions of high and low, more often then not, most people imagine bliss as an enlightened feeling, and piss as an endarkened feeling.

Desiring only love and no hate, trying to replace piss with bliss, or trying to transform bad thoughts into good thoughts which are culturally learned is a distortion of basic Buddhism. Nagarjuna states, "There is no good without bad, there is no good unrelated to bad"

The universe is composed of both. Good cannot exist without bad, just as up cannot exist without down. Trying to get rid of hate or piss in favor of love or bliss would be to paraphrase Alan Watts: "Like trying to live in a universe where there is only up and no down. There is up and down, nobody can live in just an up universe," except in a "spiritual" or "psychology" fantasy-land, called a spiritual path.

This can been viewed in an archetypical context. For example, most people either believe in God and the Devil, or they see them as two separate, independent, individual archetypes. However, when we see God and the Devil as one, to be written

God-Devil, then we can easily see that one cannot exist without the other. Once this occurs, it becomes transparent that all attempts to overcome the D-evil with God the Good, usually leaves one either in guilt, confusion or in conflict like trying to live in only an *up* universe.

"We have never had any dualistic sense experience. The sense of duality can only be thought-constructed" (Loy, 91).

Sutra xcix: Nirvana is Samsara, Samsara is Nirvana (Nagarjuna).

Commentary

Samsara has two characteristics. 1) imagining that things exist separate from other things, and 2) a world in which the "I" is experienced dualistically and is perceived as a collection of separate objects which interact causally in space-time.

Nirvana, on the other hand, can be described as the ending of the naming of all things. It is non-casual and beyond all dependence.

Nirvana is Samsara, Samsara is Nirvana (Nagarjuna). This simple statement is considered by many to be a hallmark in the Buddhist understanding. Not only is there no duality, no unity, no good or bad, both the "highest" Nirvana as well as the "lowest samsara" are acknowledged as the same. This can be likened to Advaita's "one substance" as well as Tantric yoga's "everything is consciousness" and the great statement of the Yoga Vashista, "Everything is consciousness; nothing exists outside of consciousness." With this understanding, opposites, duality, and even the concept of unity or nondualtiy, dissolve as does the illusion of spiritual qualities such as virtues or holy ideas along with the "spiritual" practices which aggrandize and attempt to cultivate these qualities as better, higher, or closer to God.

> "All spirituality and spiritual experiences are I-dependent" (post-deconstruction).

"The limits of Nirvana are the limits of Samsara. Between the two there is not the slightest difference" (Nagarjuna, Mulamadhyamakakarika XXV: 20).

If we hold this to be true, since samsara is nirvana and nirvana is samsara, then there no Nirvana or Samsara.

Another way to view the statement,
Nirvana is samsara
is that both are perceptions and as such, are not.

Sutra c: The "I" and the formation of the "I" appear as an interface between the body and the world.

Commentary

*T*he self is an effect of different natural occurrences: the molecular, bio-chemical and neurological which all organisms have.

The *subject-I* is a social creation. According to Gurdjieff, "The world is upside down." Why? Because the subject arises from the world. The subject imagines it creates or takes itself to be a stable entity which has volition, a will, choice, etc., rather than as a cultural artifact produced by the nervous system. The subject appears in an interface between the body and the world. The subject gets rigidified when the nervous system keeps producing the same subject regardless of context.

The subject-I and the experience of pres-ence are perceptual artifacts. The subject-I experiences presence, and labels and assumes it has a pre-abstraction existence, which it does not. The experience of being a *subject-I* is produced by the events of life and is composed of these events of life. Stephen Wolinsky is not a *subject-I* to whom things occurred. Rather, Stephen Wolinsky, the *subject-I* and the world are produced by a flow of events and stories or abstracted representations. The thing that must be grasped is that they are representations not *of* something or a beyond, but rather they are representations of nothing. *There is no thing that representations refer to!!!*

Sutra ci: *All "experiences" are abstractions and representational but not as representations <u>of</u> something; every experience, even the experience of present time and presence, is a representation of nothing.*

Without a perceiver perceiving there is no-thing.

Sutra cii: *The subject-I must be stripped of the illusion of its permanence, its separate existence as an individual, independent being along with the illusion that it has a creative capacity with a will, volition, and choices that exist other than as part of a language game or discourse.*

The experience of being, perceiving, and experiencing as a subject-I is the core trance.

Sutra ciii: Archetypes are copies of nothing.

Commentary

*A*rchetypes are linguistic abstracted perceived patterns which represent nothing.

To best explain archtypes, let's talk types. The use of types (or typing) is an abstracted way to categorize or territorialize behaviors in order to organize chaos. The problem is that types are an artificial, abstracted map placed over abstracted, perceived events which unfortunately act as a filter or diagnostic system whereby abstracted perceptions of people and events are squeezed into further abstracted maps or categories to make them fit. This is why oftentimes maps (types) continue to become more complicated and elaborate in an attempt to include more and more of what has been left out.

Arche(types) could simply be called the ultimate type of types, the ultimate type or category that includes people, events, or situations. We could call them the BIG Types, but more common usage today is to call them archetypes. Archetypes as BIG categories have been around since Plato and his fantasy that there is a land of perfect forms or ideas that exist in another world (the world of perfect forms). In fact, his student, Aristotle, is famous for creating categories of types in relation to animal, vegetable and mineral.

Historically, types later became a little more mystical as categories became taxonomies, whereby we not only have types, but we have types which are representative of BIG TYPES in "another world" which are more meta (beyond) physical in the land of forms where the essence of the type resides.

About 2300-2400 years after Plato, archetypes began to be referred to by such notables as anthropologist, Claude Levi-Strauss, and psychiatrist, Carl G. Jung. Levi-Strauss and others considered these types as cultural phenomena which had three purposes: 1) to reinforce cultural rituals; 2) primitive science, and 3) to explain life's contradictions.

Carl Jung seemed to go a little more along the lines of Plato, but rather than a land of perfect forms or ideas living in another world, Jung posited a collective unconscious, a meta(beyond)physical world out of which these archetypes operated. For Jung, these archetypes operate from this "other world". For post-deconstruction, Jung was both right and wrong.

First, archtypes and symbols as Levi-Strauss suggests are cultural, not universal.

Second, archetypes from a Quantum perspective are made of an interaction between the physics dimensions and forces which are perceptual representations of nothing (see *The Way of the Human Volume III*, Chapter 3, "The Collective Unconscious: The Archetypical Dimension").

Third, archetypes are abstractions, maps made of nothing.

Fourth, they do not exist as entities, but as primal organizing beliefs, or condensations of nothing.

Fifth, types are copies of archetypes, but *archetypes are abstracted perceptual representations of nothing*.

Sixth, prior to the archetypical simulation, you are *not*, and the archetype is not.

There is no need to integrate these "parts" of you as Jung insists when they are not and *you are not!!!*

Seventh, the *subject-I* is made up of the universal energies that organize in a particular way that we call archetypes. But there is no *subject-I* or archetypes that exist prior to the perceiver, which then *illusions* organizing energies.

> All archetypes are abstractions and as such are perceiver dependent.

Sutra civ: The Territorialization of Emptiness is a product of a perceiver's perception.

Commentary

All of the physical dimensions are territorializations of the emptiness which means that they appear when they are boundaried as a perception by an abstracted perceiver. Quantum Psychology calls this perception "condensations of emptiness," or "consciousness."

The misconception is that there is an "I" which does the identifying with a thought or action. The territorialization de-territorialization or condensation either happens or it doesn't.

Sutra cv: Objects in what we call the "external world" need to be viewed as "not there."

Commentary

*I*t is only through the abstraction process that an abstracted perceiver is produced without that process, neither the object nor the perceiver is there.

For a Buddhist, this can be understood as "dependent arising," emptiness becoming form, or form becoming emptiness.

Meditation, specifically in Buddhism, emphasizes the emptiness which is the other side of form or existence.

Buddhism emphasizes emptiness as a decentering of form aiding in the "understanding of dependent arising," i.e., that form and emptiness exist as part of one another (Nagarjuna).

However, *the true meaning of the Heart Sutra does not aggrandize emptiness over form,* but rather emptiness *is* form, form *is* emptiness. We could also say, **form is form, emptiness is emptiness, or emptiness is formless matter, matter is condensed emptiness.** This not only de-stabilizes the *subject-I*, but also de-stabilizes the object as both emptiness-form, form-emptiness.

A further step leads to the understanding that there is no object there, as the object is an abstraction of the perceiver. *The perceiver-perceived are both territorializations of NOTHING, or abstractions of NOTHING*, a NOTHING which is NOTHING, not a NOTHING which is a representation of a perceived NOTHING as something. Not only is the perceiver-perceived non-existent, but so is emptiness as form, form as emptiness.

This is reminiscent of **Dristi-Shristi Vada:** *"The world is there only as long as a perceiver is there to perceive it."*

Even as the witness witnesses the BIG EMPTINESS, or consciousness, when the witness "SEES" that both the witness and the emptiness (or consciousness) are made of the same substance, they both disappear. This is Sunyata which is not nothing but rather is beyond or not the nothing-something or form-emptiness.

> *"The dependent arising of all things is the realization of the absence of individual being in any person, place or thing; this is sunyata."*
> **— Nagarjuna**

Sutra cvi: *The Universe and what we call "I" are in a constant exchange, thus there is no permanent self that exists in a "now."*

Commentary

Throughout some thirteen books, the basic biological functions of eating, sleeping, shitting, fucking, learning, merging and socializing were discussed.

Noted anthropologist Claude Levi-Strauss talks of the ritual of exchange as an underlying action within culture. Even more recently, post-deconstruction isolated yet another biological function: the ***drive for stimulation.***

For us, however, this brilliant insight of Claude Levi-Strauss is merely the tip of the iceberg.

Exchange is what makes this universe, from subject to object, appear to appear.

Let's begin with a human subject taking in a breath. The body *exchanges* oxygen for carbon dioxide, then the oxygen is *exchanged* for energy which metabolizes food, then the body excretes "waste", which plants *exchange* for food.

At an atomic level too, electrons spin off (*exchange*) to form other atoms and molecules. It can be said that on the level of phenomenon, the universe is in a constant *exchange* forming what we call the "I." This underlying *exchange* process is the interconnected one universe at work.

It is for this reason that although a **subject-I** appears to appear, nevertheless, it is formed through *exchanges*, giving the illustion of a permanent self, living in a "now".

This is not dissimilar from the Madhyamika's doctrine of "dependent arising." With everything in exchange and harmony with everything else, there can be no separate independent subject.

Sutra cvii: All perceivables and conceivables are not.

Commentary

Since all perceivables and conceivables are abstractions of nothing, then neither are without an abstracted perceiver to perceive them.

Sutra cviii: All theories of spirituality are theories, representations and metaphors. Since they are metaphorical representations based on an abstracted imagined subject-I, all spiritual theories and practices are fiction.

Commentary

Spiritual paths are theories based on concepts, precepts, representations and words which are sounds. It is of no surprise that the Zen Koan, "What is the sound of one hand clapping?" attempts to lead "us" through inquiry into this "understanding/experience." The importance is that there are no paths prior to words, and no philosophy of being or presence before or without the abstraction process which yields words. Is there a psychology, spirituality or presence? Yes, in abstracted words only, but one hand clapping is not in words. Can a path lead beyond or prior to words?

Yes, if the words are deconstructed and seen as an illusion of the nervous system as we go along.

The importance is that words that are sounds are abstracted representations. As representations, they are representations of nothing, not of something. Therefore, all words/sounds that represent nothing are metaphors, or more directly, fictions. Therefore, **what a *subject-I* experiences as spiritual, or a psychological presence or present, requires an abstracted experiencer. Therefore, all experiences from the mundane to the spiritual, from the psychological to the experience of presence require an experiencer to experience them. Once the experiencer and the experience are seen as the same substance, they both disappear. All experiences are a fiction because they are perceiver dependent and a** representation not of something, but of nothing.

There is no true world beyond or prior to the abstracted perceiver of sound or words.

Sutra cix: The soul is a metaphor that represents a subject-I's delusion.

Commentary

*T*he soul incarnating from body to body or from lifetime to lifetime is a metaphor of the body decaying and dying, being eaten by micro-organisms and worms, etc . Part of the body gets turned into fertilizer to be eaten by a tree or plant, part into shit which helps a tree to grow fruit and be eaten. This never-ending cycle is not individual, and since there is only one substance in nature and sub-atomically, it requires a *perceiver-I* to separate and see one subatomic particle as being separate from another subatomic particle. Everything is in constant change with no individual separate self-nature.

All language and perceptions are metaphors. All abstracted representations, archetypes and logo-centric stories are metaphors.

The concept of a *subject-I* conjures up a meta-phoric representation which is experienced as a fact which justifies its metaphorical existence. This attempt by the *subject-I* to exist and have significance is a resistance to this simple understanding. *The illusion is that the subject-I not only exists, but that it will continue to exist in some invisible form called a soul.*

"Why then," some ask, "at the time of death, is this felt palatable presence not a soul?"

It is an expansion of a de-territorialized representation of life moving from its contracted to its expanded state, like air in a bottle would if the bottle is broken.

The above hopefully deconstructs the soul metaphor.

Epilogue

*H*ow does one end a text such as *The Nirvana Sutras* other than to summarize where we have been and to deconstruct even the Nirvana Sutras?

Summary

- The "I" and for that matter all words are representations, abstractions of nothing without an independent separate existence prior to the nervous system. The great illusion is that there is a separate, independent, individual "I" which exists, and which does not occur through the movement of fluids called neuro-transmitters. This abstracted I AM appears and gives words and perceptions the illusion of existence, and the "I" and the "other" the illusion of being.

- All experiences are abstractions, and as such they are perceptions, thus experiences carry with them **the illusion of a separate, individual, independent being, presence or self which is contained within the experience.**

- This perceptual, experiential game gives the illusion of things and/or ideas which exist outside of an abstracted perceivers' perceptions and which contain a separate, independent, individual self nature.

- In Buddhism, everything is inter-dependent and *dependently arising*, and therefore has no separate, individual, independent presence, self-nature or existence; hence, all things *as separate, individual, independent things* do not exist. They are void or empty of a separate, individual, self-nature with a separate will, volition or choices, because they do not exist as separate individual entities.

- The "I" and even the feeling of "I" as subject is an abstraction, a word, and all words carry their meanings in relationship to other words. For us, words are representations of objects, and as abstractions that not only have no existence outside of their use, function or relationship, but moreover, as representations/abstractions they represent nothing which actually exists outside of a perceiver.

- All meanings placed on perception and experiences are derived from cultural learning, information and thought passed down from generations. The meaning placed on perceptions and experiences occurs after the perception or experience has already occurred.

- "Spirituality" and a personal psychology exist in language only as part of a system of words or signs which Wittgenstein calls a *language game*. All perceptions and meanings, like "this is spiritual," "this is not spiritual," "this is healthy" or "appropriate" are arbitrary, learned and cultural. As such, they are and exist in language as information or knowledge and should be discarded as **NOT THIS.**

- Casual connections are abstractions the nervous system superimposes on the world which the "I" "experiences."

- There is no difference between the content of consciousness and consciousness itself. They are both made of the same substance.

- In order for there to be cause and effect, there would have to be two separate and distinct entities which would mean there is more than one substance and no dependent arising.

- Nisargadatta Maharaj said, "There is no gain and there is no loss." The idea of gaining or getting something and the fear of losing something, even a state of consciousness, is a repetitive pattern of an "I" who does something in order to get something, or who avoids doing something so as not to lose something. These concepts are culturally derived (like being "good" and not being "bad") and are later transposed or superimposed on "spirituality" and a personal "psychology" as rules, a path or codes of behavior in order to achieve a permanent state of pleasure and no pain, which some call "enlightenment."

- There is no authority outside or inside that can give or transmit something which you are not already. Both "outer" and "inner" are made of the same consciousness. When Nisargadatta said, " Your own Self is the guru, for it is your own Self which walks with you to your goal," he meant you are that Self, or consciousness, not some separate deity that is not you, which, if you are good and do what you are supposed to, like you were brought up, then you will get this reward called permanent pleasure and not pain.

- There is no inner self, higher self or *big I* that is separate from *the Self* or consciousness which teaches lessons or has an agenda for you. The concept of an inner self, a higher self, a witness and even awareness all imply two or more substances. These "states" are still constructions of consciousness, and as such they must be deconstructed.

- "The dependent arising of all things is the absence of being"(Nagarjuna). For spirituality to exist outside of language and the abstraction process would require that something exist outside an abstracted perceiver. However, since *spirituality is "I" dependent* then *there is no "spirituality" that exists separate from the "I" we call ego*. If there is no spirituality outside of abstraction/representation/language and the "I" is abstracted and in language only, then all principles and paths have no existence outside of, beyond, or behind abstractions and words.

- Since everything has dependent origination and arises dependent upon everything else, then there is no separate self or presence with volition, a will, choices or personal karma. Hence, if the self is defined as an independent, separate, individual entity and it is not, then the self is empty of self-existence and is non-existent.

Summary of The Illusionary Trap of the "I" Word

- Words derive their meaning only through their reference to other words, and have no meaning in and of themselves.

- There is no "I," "other" or "knower" which exists outside of an abstracted word/map.

- The "I" (as all words) is dependent upon other words and refers to other words in order to derive its meaning. As in Buddhism, there is no independent, separate thing, so too in language there is no independent separate words that have a self nature (meaning or existence) as an independent entity.

- The "I" as an abstracted, arbitrary representation, has no existence outside of language. The word "I" as well as the objects which words represent carry with them give the **illusion of being an imaginary presence or an existence outside of the abstraction/perception process as independent and separate entities.**

- The *subject-I* arises after the event or action has already taken place, and then assumes do-ership, as if it chose or created its actions or perceptions. Since the perception of anything requires both an abstraction as well as a representation, then anything perceived along with the perceiver is an abstracted representation of nothing.

Deconstructing the Approaches

Dristi Shristi Vada: *The world is only there as long as there is an "I" there to perceive it.*

- "The dependent arising of all things is the absence of an individual being in them; this is sunyata" (Nagarjuna).

- The perceptions of a body, a world, an event, present time, a presence, the survival mechanism and even a nervous system, a *subject-I*, space-time, location, the void, emptiness or even the one substance are perceptions. All experiences requiring an experiencer, abstracted representation and conclusions of the nervous system, and as such are all illusions.

- There is no dependent arising or dependent origination that exists outside of a perceiver's perception. Dependent arising is therefore only a "tool" of understanding to be discarded.

- The "I" or self can be viewed (as a abstract representation by a perceiver) as an interaction of the five skandhas of Buddhism, as the five elements and three gunas of Yoga, or an interaction of the physics dimensions and forces in Quantum Psychology. Regardless, the "I" does not have an independent, separate individual nature in and of itself; hence, its nature is empty (is not). Even the perception of the skandas, the elements and the physics dimensions and forces are perceptions. They, too, are "tools" which as abstractions/perceptions are not.

- Form is emptiness; emptiness is also form. Emptiness is none other than form; form is no other than emptiness. This is a perceptual, verbal "understanding." Neither form nor emptiness as an abstracted perception is actually a separate independent "thing" outside of a perceiver's perception.

- Nirvana is samsara, samsara is nirvana. You cannot have only an "up" universe. You cannot have one without the other. Since they negate each other, like form and emptiness, neither is.

This is why the Buddha said, "Those who seek Nirvana are ignorant, those who seek samsara are ignorant." Why? Because samsara is Nirvana, Nirvana is samasara. Neither are.

• Feeling, perception, and consciousness are empty of an individual independent separate self nature and dharmas and paths are empty as perceptual conclusions.

> *Forsake All Dharmas*
> **— Buddha**

Appendix I

Describing "What is Left" or Post-Deconstruction

For more than 2500 years, people have been trying to describe in words what *no-I* is like. Below are some attempts, some through affirmation, others through negation.

The Way of Truth, Parmenides (approximately 500-600 B.C.)

It is ungenerated and indestructible.
No distinctions can be made within it.
The whole is full of continuous being.
There is no generation or destruction;
hence, no motion or change.

The Eight Negations of Nagarjuna

1. Nothing arises, nothing is created, and nothing is born.

2. Nothing subsides, nothing is eliminated, and nothing dies.

3. Nothing ceases to exist, or can be destroyed.

4. There is no beginning, there is no end

5. Nothing is the same as anything else, there is no unity.

6. Nothing is different from anything else, no duality.

7. Nothing arises, or comes

8. Nothing subsides, leaves, departs or goes.

Nisargadatta Maharaj

- There are no characteristics. There is no birth and o cessation. There is no impurity and no purity. There is no decrease and no increase, and there is no gain, there is no loss.

"There is no birth, there is no death.
There is no person.
It is all a concept.
It is all an illusion."

This deconstructs even 8 limb yoga, leaving us beyond the Dharana (concentration practice) of "limb," "step," or "fold 6" in Raja Yoga, or beyond the Buddhist "8 fold path," beyond ""step," "limb" or "fold 8" in Raja yoga, or Buddhist "8 fold" yoga called Samadhi or perfect concentration respectively, and into "step," "limb" or "fold 9, which is not." This is *no-"I" realization* when the focuser, witness, awarer, knower, observer is "seen" as the same energy or consciousness as the witnessed, awared, known, or observed. This is what Nisargadatta Maharaj called unawareness, this is the Nisarga: *The Natural Yoga.*

Appendix II

Where Does This Leave Post-Deconstruction?

- There is no individual mind. only one mind which is consciousness itself.

- There is no mind, as the mind is a metaphor, an abstracted representation of nothing.

- The "I" cannot know this consciousness directly as this "I" is a condensation of that consciousness.

- There is no substratum or ground; all is empty of a separate , individual, independent beingness.

- the self or consciousness cannot be known, for to know it would be to make consciousness into an object and would require a separate substance to say, "Ah, that is consciousness."

In whatever form it takes, from the most gross "I" to the most subtle witness, knower, or awarer that wants to see or experience, the no-I, is the last to dissolve.

Baba Prakashananda once said to me, "You don't want liberation because if you have it you won't be there to appreciate it." An "I" can never know it is enlightened.

There is no spirituality or personal psychology.
All spirituality and psychology are "I" dependent.
With No-I there no spirituality and
no personal psychology,
and
With No-"I" there is No post-deconstruction.

You are the child of a barren woman.
— Nisargadatta Maharaj

With love,
Your Mirage brother,
Stephen

Appendix III

Summary of the 133 Illusions of Consciousness

1.   The illusion that you are

2.   the illusion of a self

3.   the illusion of a soul

4.   the illusion of a present time

5.   the illusion of presence

6.   the illusion of Nirvana

7.   the illusion of heaven

8.   the illusion of being

9.   the illusion of a separate individual subject-I

10.   the illusion of a witness

11.   the illusion of an awarer

12.   the illusion of an observer

13.   the illusion of a knower

14.   the illusion of a known

15.   the illusion of nothing

16.   the illusion of something

17.   the illusion of enlightenenment

18.   the illusion of existence

19.   the illusion of non-existence

20.   the illusion of location

21.   the illusion of cause

22.   the illusion of an effect

23.   the illusion of cause-effect

24.   the illusion past-time

25.   The illusion of present-time

26.   The illusion of future-time

27.   the illusion of energy

28.   the illusion of space

29.   the illusion of time

30.   the illusion of form or solidness

31.   the illusion of distance

32.   the illusion of a path

33.   the illusion of "the substance"

34.   the illusion of God

35.   the illusion of spirituality

36.   the illusion of death

37.   the illusion of psychology

38.   the illusion of arising

39.   the illusion of subsiding

40.   the illusion of coming

41.   the illusion of going

42.   the illusion of sameness

43.   the illusion of differences

44.   the illusion of spiritual practices

45. the illusion of a personal psychology
46. The illusion of a collective unconscious
47. the illusion of consciousness
48. the illusion of dependent origination
49. the illusion of origination, sourcing, or creating
50. the illusion of dharma
51. the illusion of air
52. The illusion of earth
53. the illusion of water
54. the illusion of fire
55. the illusion of ether
56. the illusion of a body
57. the illusion of a nervous system
58. the illusion of reasons
59. the illusion of hope
60. the illusion of whole(s)
61. the illusion of continuity
62. the illusion of mind
63. the illusion of subatomis particles
64. the illusion of forces
65. the illusion of inertia
66. the illusion of activity
67. the illusion of purity

68. the illusion of truth

69. the illusion of "getting it"

70. the illusion of enlightenment

71. the illusion of electromagnetics

72. the illusion of gravity

73. the illusion of light

74. the illusion of sound

75. the illusion of strong force

76. the illusion of a werk force

77. the illusion of a perceiver

78. the illusion of a survival mechanism

79. the illusion of a logos

80. the illusion of permanence

81. the illusion of impermanence

82. the illusion of a mission

83. the illusion of a purpose

84. the illusion of choice

85. the illusion of a gift

86. the illusion of a calling

87. the illusion of an origin

88. the illusion of virtue

89. the illusion of sin

90. the illusion of spiritual principles, acts, behaviors, feelings, experiences or states

91.   the illusion of doership

92.   the illusion of authorship

93.   the illusion of sayership

94.   the illusion of volition

95.   the illusion of will

96.   the illusion of motives,(motivations)

97.   the illusion of reasons

98.   the illusion of creation

99.   the illusion of destruction

100.   the illusion of elimination

101.   the illusion of eternal or eternity

102.   the illusion of constancy

103.   the illusion of karma

104.   the illusion of lessons

105.   the illusion of reincarnation

106.   the illusion of patterns

107.   the illusion of archetypes

108.   the illusion of fluid

109.   the illusion of movement

110.   the illusion of pleasant

111.   the illusion of unpleasant

112.   the illusion of neutral

113.   the illusion of sound

114.   the illusion of smell

115. the illusion of taste

116. the illusion of bodily impressions

117. the illusion of volition

118. the illusion of attention

119. the illusion of discrimination

120. the illusion of joy

121. the illusion of happiness

122. the illusion of equanimity

123. the illusion of resolve

124. the illusion of exertion

125. the illusion of compulsion

126. the illusion of concentration

127. the illusion of seeing

128. the illusion of hearing

129. the illusion of smelling

130. the illusion of tasting

131. the illusion of bodily sensation

132. the illusion of mental consciousness

133. *the illusion of there being an illusion*

Bibliography

* *Indicates important to read.*

American College Dictionary. (1963). New York: Random House.

Aranja, H. (1983). *Yoga philosophy of Patanjali.* Albany, NY: State University of New York Press.

Audi, R., (Ed.). *The Cambridge dictionary of philosophy.* (1995, 1999). Cambridge, England: Cambridge University Press.

Ayer, A. J. (1946). *Language, truth and logic.* Dover, England.

Bahirjit, B. B. (1963). *The Amritanubhava of Janadeva.* Bombay: Sirun Press.

*Balsekar, R. (1982). *Pointers from Nisargadatta Maharaj.* Durham, NC: Acorn Press.

Baudrillard, J. (1983). *Simulations* (Nicola Dufresre, Trans.). New York: Semio Text.

Bentov, I. (1977). *Stalking the wild pendulum.* Rochester, Vermont: Destiny Books.

Berman, D. (1998). *The world as will and representation* (abridged). Dover, Charles, England: Tuttle Press.

Bohm, D. (1951). *Quantum theory.* London: Constable.

-------- (1980). *Wholeness and the implicit order.* London: Ark Paperbacks.

Bois, J. S. (1978). *The art of awareness: A textbook on general semantics and epistemics* (3rd ed.). Dubuque, IA: William C. Brown Company.

*Buddha. (1969). *Diamond sutra.* (A. F. Price & M.-L. Wong, trans.). Boulder, CO: Shambhala.

*Buddhist Text Translation Society. (1980). *The heart sutra and commentary.* San Francisco: Buddhist Text Translation Society.

The Cambridge guide to early Greek philosophy. (1981). Cambridge, England: Cambridge University Press.

Camus, A. (1955). *The myth of Sisyphus and other essays,* New York, NY: Alfred A. Knopf.

Cane, R. J. (2000). *Jean Baudrillard.* New York: Routledge.

*Capra, F. (1976). *The tao of physics.* New York: Bantam Books.

*Chisholm, F. P. (1945). *Introductory lectures on general semantics.* Brooklyn, NY: Institute of General Semantics.

Coward, H. (1990). *Derrida and Indian philosophy* (p. 61). Albany, NY: State University of New York.

Coward, H. G., & Kunjunmi Raja, K. (1990). *The philosophy of the Grammarians.* Princeton, NJ: Princeton University Press.

Cullen, Johnathan (1982). *On Reconstruction: A Theory and Criticism after Structuralism.* Cornell Univ. Press, Ithaca, NY.

Dawkins, R. (1978). *The selfish genes.*

Davison, R. (1997). *Camus: The challenge of Dostoyevsky,* Devon, England: University of Exeter Press.

Dostoyevsky, F.   *The brothers Karamazov* (pp. 255-274). New York: Modern Library.

*Dunn, J. (Ed.). (1982). *Seeds of consciousness.* New York, NY: Grove Press.

*-------- (1985). *Prior to consciousness.* Durham, NC: Acorn Press.

*-------- (1994). Consciousness and the absolute. Durham, NC: Acorn Press.

Edinger, E. (1992). *Ego and the archetype: Individualization and the religious function of the archetype.* Boston, MA: Shambhala.

Edwards, P. (Ed.). (1967). *The encyclopedia of philosophy* (eight volumes). New York/ London: Macmillan Publishing Co., and The Free Press, Colliere Macmillan Publishers.

Encyclopedia of eastern philosophy and religion. (1989). Boston, MA: Shambala Press.

*Genova, J. (1991). *Wittgenstein: A way of seeing.* New York: Routledge.

Gleick, J. (1987). *Chaos.* New York: Penguin Books.

Glock, H.-J. (1996). *Wittgenstein dictionary* (pp. 193-196). Malden, MA: Blackwelle.

*Godman, D. (1985). *The teaching of Ramana Maharishi.* London: Ankara.

Gregory, R. L. (1970). *The intelligent eye.* New York: McGraw-Hill.

Gregory, R. L. (1978). *Eye and brain: The psychology of seeing* (3rd ed.). New York: McGraw-Hill.

Hawking, S. (1988). *A brief history of time.* New York: Bantam Books.

Hayakawa, S. I. (1978). *Language in thought and action* (4th ed.). New York: Harcourt, Brace, Jovanovich.

Heidegger, M. (2000). *Introduction to metaphysics* (R. Polk & G. Fried, Eds.). New Haven-Cordon, CT: Yale University Press.

Heidegger, M. (2001). *A companion to Heidegger's Introduction to Metaphysics* (R. Polk & G. Fried, Eds.). New Haven-Cordon, CT: Yale University Press.

Hopkins, J. (1987). *Emptiness yoga: The Tibetan middle way*. Ithaca, NY: Snow Lion Press.

Hua, T. (1980). *Surangama sutra*. San Francisco: Buddhist Text Translation Society.

Hume, D. (1883). *An inquiry concerning human understanding*. Indianapolis, IN: Hackett.

Ichazo, O. (1993). *The fourteen pillars of perfect recognition*. New York: The Arica Institute.

Isherwood, C., & Prhnavarla, S. (1953). *How to know God: The yoga of Patanjali*. CA: New American Library.

*Iyer, R. (Ed.). (1983). *The diamond sutra*. New York: Concord Grove Press.

James, W. (1994). *Varieties of religious experience*. New York: Modern Library.

Janssen, G. E. (Ed.). (1962). *Selections from science and sanity*. Brooklyn, NY: Institute of General Semantics.

Jnaneshwar. (1969). *Jnaneshwari, a song-sermon on the Bhagavad Gita*. Bombay, India: Blackie & Sons Publishers.

Kaku, M. (1987). *Beyond Einstein: The cosmic quest for the theory of the universe*. New York: Bantam.

-------- (1994). *Hyperspace*. New York: Anchor-Doubleday.

Kaufmann, W. (1954). *The portable Nietzsche*. New York: Penguin Books.

King, M. A. (2001). *Guide to Heidegger's Being and Time*. (J. Llewelyn, Ed.). Albany, NY: State University of New York.

Korzybski, A. (1947). *Historical note on the structural differential* (audiotape). Brooklyn, NY: Institute of General Semantics. The text of this audiotape appears in *Alfred Korzybski:*

Collected Writings: 1920-1950 (M. Kendig, Ed.). Brooklyn, NY: Institute of General Semantics, 1990.

-------- (1993). Science and sanity: An introduction to non-aristotelian systems and general semantics (5th ed.). Brooklyn, NY: Institute of General Semantics.

Krishnamurti, U. G. (1984). *The mystique of enlightenment: The unrational ideas of a man called U.G.* New York: Coleman.

-------- (1988). The mind is myth: Disquieting conversations with the man called U.G. India: Dinesh Publications.

-------- (1997). The courage to stand alone. New York: Plover Press.

Levi-Strauss, C. (1974). *Structural anthropology* (C. Jackson, Trans.). New York: Penguin Books.

Long, A. A. (Ed.). (1999). *The Cambridge companion to early Greek philosophy*. Cambridge, England: Cambridge University Press.

Lopez, Jr., D. S. (1988). *The heart sutra explained.* Albany, NY: State University of New York Press.

Loy, David, (1988). *Nonduality: A study of comparative philosophy*. Humanities Press, New Jersey.

*Lyotard, J. F. (1982). *The postmodern condition.* Minneapolis, MN: University of Minnesota.

Macy, D. (2000). *The Cambridge dictionary of critical theory*. London, England: Penguin Books.

Markos, L. (1999). *From Plato to postmodernism: Glossary and bibliography*. Chantilly, VA: The Teaching Company.

Marx, K. (1872). *The essential writings*. New York: F. Bender.

McHoul, A., & Grace, W. (1993). *A Foucault primer: Discourse, power, and the subject*. New York: New York University Press.

Mishra, R. S. (1968). *The textbook of yoga psychology of Patanjali's yoga sutras in all modern psychological disciplines*. New York: Julian Press/Crown Press.

Monk, R. (1990). *Ludwig Wittgenstein: The duty of genius* (J. Cape, Ed.). London: Penguin.

Mookerjit, A. (1971). *Tantra asana. A way to self-realization*. Basel, Switzerland: Ravi Kumar.

Mueller, C. G. (1965). *Sensory psychology*. Englewood Cliffs, NJ: Prentice-Hall, Inc.

Mulhall, S. (1996). *Routledge philosophy guidebook to Heidegger's Being and Time*. New York: Routledge.

Natoli, J. (1997). *A primer to postmodernity*, Malden, MA: Blackwelle.

Nietzsche, F. (1967). *Will to Power* (W. Kaufmann & R.J. Hollinsdale, Trans.). New York: Vintage Books.

Nietzsche, F. (1968). *Basic writing of Nietzsche*. (W. Kaufmann & R. J. Hollinsdale, Trans.). New York: Modern Library.

*Nisargadatta M. (1973). *I am that*. Durham, NC: Acorn Press.

Orage, A. R. (1974). *On love*. New York: Samuel Weiser.

*Osborne, A. (1960). *The collected works of Ramana Maharishi*, York Beach, ME: Samuel Weiser.

Ouspensky, P. D. (1949). *In search of the miraculous*. New York: Harcourt, Brace and World.

Plato. (1937). *The Dialogues of Plato* (B. Jowett, Trans.). New York: Random House.

Plato. (1937). *The Republic in Dialogues of Plato* (B. Jowett, Trans.). New York: Random House.

Poona, S. I. (1969). *Bhartrhari*. Poona, India: Deccan College.

*Powell, R. (Ed.). (1987) *The nectar of the Lord's feet.* England: Element Books. (Published in 1997 as *The nectar of immortality.* San Diego, CA: Blue Dove Press.)

*-------- (1994). The ultimate medicine. San Diego, CA: Blue Dove Press.

*-------- (1996). The experience of nothingness. San Diego, CA: Blue Dove Press.

*Pula, R. P. (1979). *General semantics seminar.* San Diego, CA: Educational Cassettes. (Album IV-D: set of six audiotapes distributed by the Institute of General Semantics).

Ree, J., & Chamberlain, J. (Eds.). (1998). *Kierkegaard: A critical reader.* Oxford, England: Blackwell.

Rosenau, P. M. (1992). *Postmodernism and the social sciences.* Princeton, NJ: Princeton University Press.

Russell, B. (1961). *The basic writings of Bertrand Russell.* New York: Simon & Schuster.

de Saussure, Ferdinand. (1966). *The course in general linguistics* (W. Baskin, Trans.). New York.

*Sawin, G. (2002-2003). The structural differential diagram. In *Et cetera: A Review of General Semantics, 59*(4) (Winter 2002); *60*(1) (Spring 2003); *60*(2) (Summer 2003); and *60*(3) (Fall

2003). Concord, CA: International Society for General Semantics.

Schulte, J. (1992). *Wittgenstein: An introduction.* State University of New York Press.

Shah, I. (1978). *Learning how to learn: Psychology and spirituality in the Sufi way.* San Francisco: Harper & Row.

*Singh, J. (1963). *Pratyabhijnahrdayam: The secret of self recognition.* Delhi, India: Motilal Banarsidass.

*-------- (1979). Siva sutra: The yoga of supreme identity. Delhi, India: Motilal Banarsidass.

*-------- (1979). Vijnanabhairava: Divine consciousness. Delhi, India: Motilal Banarsidass.

*-------- (1980). Spanda karikas: Lessons in the divine pulsation. Delhi, India: Motilal Banarsidass.

Spinoza, B. (1957). *The ethics of Spinoza.* New York: Citadel Press.

*Spinoza, B. (1994). *The Ethics and other works.* Princeton, NJ: Princeton University Press.

Sprintzen, D. (1988). *Camus: A critical examination.* Philadelphia: Temple University Press.

Staten, H. (1982). *Wittgenstein and Derrida.* Oxford, England: Blackwell.

Suzuki, S. (1970). *Zen mind, beginner's mind.* New York: Weatherhill.

*Taimini, I. K. (1961). *The science of yoga.* Wheaton, IL: Theosophical Publishing House.

Talbot, M. (1987). *Beyond the quantum.* New York: Bantam Books.

Venkatesananda, S. (1976). *The supreme yoga.* Melbourne, Australia: Chiltern Yoga Trust.

*Weinberg, H. L. (1959). *Levels of knowing and existence: Studies in general semantics.*

Brooklyn, NY: Institute of General
Semantics.

Weiss, T. M., Moran, E. V., & Cottle, E. (1975). *Education for adaptation and survival.* San Francisco: International Society for General Semantics.

Wittgenstein, L. (1969). *On certainty.* Oxford, England: Blackwell.

*Wittgenstein, L. (1958). *Philosophical investigations.* Oxford, England: Blackwell.

*Wittgenstein, L. (1958). *The blue and brown books.* New York: Harper & Row, New York.

Wolinsky, S. H. (1991). *Trances people live: Healing approaches to quantum psychology.* Norfolk, CT: Bramble Co.

*-------- (1993). Quantum consciousness. Norfolk, CT: Bramble Books.

-------- (1993). The dark side of the inner child. Norfolk, CT: Bramble Co.

-------- (1994). The tao of chaos: Quantum consciousness (Vol. II). Norfolk, CT: Bramble Books.

-------- (1995). Hearts on fire: The tao of meditation. Capitola, CA: Quantum Institute.

-------- (1999). The way of the human, Vol. I. Capitola, CA: Quantum Institute.

-------- (1999). The way of the human, Vol. II. Capitola, CA: Quantum Institute.

*-------- (1999). The way of the human, Vol. III. Capitola, CA: Quantum Institute.

*-------- (2000). I am that I am: A tribute to Sri Nisargadatta Maharaj. Capitola, CA: Quantum Institute.

-------- (2000). Intimate relationships: Why they do and do not work. Capitola, CA: Quantum Institute.

*-------- (2002). YOU ARE NOT: Beyond the three veils of consciousness. Capitola, CA: Quantum Institute.

*-------- (2003). Walden III: In Search of a Utopia Nirvana. Aptos, CA: Quantum Institute.

I AM THAT I AM
EXPERIENCING THE TEACHINGS
OF SRI NISARGADATTA MAHARAJ

In December 2004, documentary film maker Maurizo Benazzo will release a new DVD-CD set containing never before seen footage of Sri Nisargadatta Maharaj. Narrated by Dr. Stephen Wolinsky this three hour DVD-CD set will contain not only The Complete Teachings of Sri Nisargadatta Maharaj, but also "experiential meditations" to lead the viewer into the I AM, and beyond, into That One Substance from which all phenomena appear to arise

The DVD-CD set will provide an in-depth discussion of the Essence of the Teachings of Sri Nisargadatta Maharaj and their relationship to Buddhism, Science, Advaita-Vedanta, The I AM, The Body, Consciousness, The Nothingness, Realization, Spirituality and Spiritual Paths, The Guru, The Void, Birth and Death, Cause and Effect, That One Substance, and The Illusion.

For details about ordering
please contact after November 2004:
mauriziobenazzo@hotmail.com
or shwolinsky@mac.com